Giuseppe's Recipes

Giuseppe's Recipes

An Adventure With a Fork

To

Mark Crosby

Bon Appetit

Joe Colistro

Written by Joseph Colistro

The greatest chef the world has
never known

authorHOUSE®

AuthorHouse™
1663 Liberty Drive
Bloomington, IN 47403
www.authorhouse.com
Phone: 1-800-839-8640

Published by AuthorHouse   06/18/2013

ISBN: 978-1-4817-5727-0 (sc)
ISBN: 978-1-4817-5726-3 (hc)
ISBN: 978-1-4817-3985-6 (e)

Library of Congress Control Number: 2013909950

TABLE OF CONTENTS

Soups

Side Dishes and Sauces

Main Courses

Wild Game

Upland Birds, Chickens, and Ducks

Seafood

Pasta and Rice Dishes

"That Was Good! What is it?!"

Bread, Bannock, Biscuits, and Dough

Desserts

Smoked Meats and fish

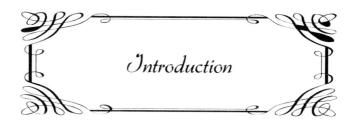

Introduction

In the song Fruit Cakes, sung by Jimmy Buffet, a line says, "There's a fine line between Saturday night and Sunday Morning". Well Jimmy Buffet may have sung about it, but my parents lived it. Growing up in the 1960s the first rule of weekends was don't wake up Momma. But when this six-year-old got hungry, I would sneak in and making sure I was out of reach I would sneak up on the bed, and in a soft voice I would ask. "Momma what's for breakfast"? At first only Mom's breathing would alter, then her arm would come out from under the covers with her fingers curled into claws and start sweeping back and forth and the first words were always! "Well, let's just say if you were to hear what she said, you would know that she was the daughter of a steel worker".

Then when she realized I was out of reach, mom would open an eye and look over at me and say, "If you want breakfast, go make it." And make it I did.

I grew up in an Italian/hillbilly family. Dad did most of the cooking, and besides teaching my two sisters and I how to cook, he also ran a catering business. Dad's dream was to open a restaurant which he finally did "Joe's Warehouse".

From an early age I was introduced to hunting and fishing. The first rule was safety; the second rule was do not kill anything you are not prepared to eat. Both rules were strictly enforced, and by the age of ten, I learned I liked Blue Jays better than Robins, although both went well in tomato sauce.

Growing up I had several friends of varied nationalities. The one thing I noticed was how they adapted their family and cultural recipes to the local foods that were available. When their moms made something I liked I learned how to make it.

After High School I joined the United States Navy and traveled half way around the world. Not only did I enjoy some great meals, but I also learned from the locals how to cook them.

So from these humble beginnings I started cooking, and over the years I have created and collected recipes. The origins and styles you will see are as varied as the world we live in and to me, that is has it should be. I hope you enjoy these recipes

I dedicate this book to my Mom, Dad and my family and friends.

Art work Acknowledgement:

I thank my mother Alora Colistro for the exterior artwork and my extremely talented cousin Bonnie Junell for the interior art work.

Eggs and Things
in the Morning

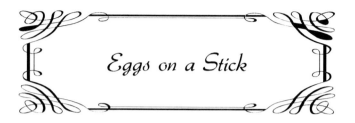

Eggs on a Stick

In High School, my buddies and I often camped and fished on Mt. Hood. Most of the time, we would head up the mountain with just a couple of boxes of frozen chicken and eat it when it was thawed out, fish all day and head home. On one of those trips, I decided to bring some eggs for breakfast and it was one of those camping trips where things were forgotten, like the pots and pans! Thank God for the Boy Scout Manual.

4 eggs
½ pound butter chilled
2-3 cups very fine breadcrumbs (about 8 slices of bread.)

Beat the eggs until nice and frothy. Form the chilled butter into a ball, roll it in breadcrumbs, then in eggs, and repeat this until all of the breadcrumbs and eggs have been absorbed. Put the ball on the end of a sharpened stick or spit and cook slowly over very dark coals until it is crisply browned, about 15 to 20 minutes. Don't laugh—it works and tastes pretty good.

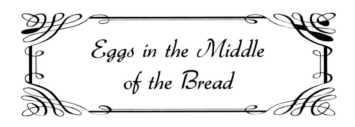

Eggs in the Middle of the Bread

This is the recipe that started me on my way to cooking.

Eggs
Bread
Butter

Take a slice of bread and tear a 1-2" inch hole out of the middle, butter the face of the bread and place into a heated skillet butter side down. Cut butter into small pieces and place on the corners of the bread then crack an egg into the hole. Turn over when bread is browned on the bottom and the egg is firm in the hole, cook for about 1-2 minutes more and serve. Allow two per person. This is a great breakfast when camping or hunting and there isn't toaster.

Shepherd's Pie

This is a great dish to cook when you are feeding a lot of people or just need to clean out the cooler.

6 eggs
1 cup cream or milk
½ pound of meat (sausage, bacon, steak, ham, Spam or any combination thereof)
3 potatoes
1 yellow onion
Grated cheese

If using meat that needs to be cooked place meat into a heated pan and cook it. Once cooked, remove to a casserole dish, dice the potatoes and place into a heated pan with enough oil to cover the bottom. When potatoes are ¾ of the way done, add the cut up onion. ***If using meat that is already cooked, add it now.*** Remove from pan and add to the casserole dish. Beat eggs together with milk and add grated cheese, pour into casserole dish and place some more cheese on top. Place into the oven at 375 degrees and cook for 30-40 minutes. Check the middle for doneness, heat until the middle is no longer runny.

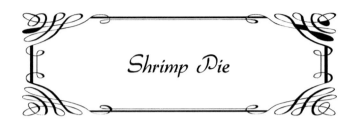

Shrimp Pie

1-pound large shrimp cooked, deveined and peeled
½ pound fresh asparagus
½ sweet yellow onion
¼ lb. Canadian bacon
3 red potatoes
12 eggs
½ cream or milk
1 cup Swiss cheese, shredded
Hollandaise sauce
Butter

In a large skillet, heat 1 tablespoon of butter and 2 tablespoons olive oil. Add chopped potatoes and cook until browned, then add onion and cook until onions are clear. While the potatoes are cooking, preheat oven to 350 degrees and place a 9x13" casserole dish that has been rubbed with butter into the oven. When potatoes are cooked, add to the casserole dish. Add the asparagus to the skillet and cook for about 3 minutes. Add chopped Canadian bacon and chopped shrimp and cook for another 2 minutes. In the meantime, add eggs to a large bowl. Beat and add ½ cup of cream and mix. Remove the casserole from the oven add asparagus mixture into the potatoes and mix well. Add the eggs and cheese (mixing well) then place back into the oven for 35 minutes or until the center is cooked. Make the hollandaise sauce; cut the pie into serving size pieces, and plate with the hollandaise sauce on top.

Hangtown Fry

For 1 person

3 eggs
2 Tbs. cream
6 oysters, steamed or left over from an oyster feed the night before
2 slices bacon
Swiss cheese
1-cup fresh spinach
Hollandaise sauce

Cook bacon and remove from pan, beat eggs and cream together and pour into a medium heated pan. Once the egg is firm, lay Swiss cheese on one side of the omelet, place the oysters on top of the cheese, crumble the bacon onto the other side, and lay the fresh spinach on top. After about 2-3 minutes, gently fold the bacon side over onto the oyster side. Cook for about 2 more minutes or until eggs are no longer runny and gently flip onto a plate. Cover with Hollandaise sauce and serve.

Lobster and Chanterelle Omelet

Serves 4-6 people. The secret to this is to have everything separated and ready before you start making the omelets. Ladle the eggs into the sauté pan to make individual omelets.

1 pound cooked or frozen lobster
1 pound sliced chanterelle mushrooms
12 eggs
½ cup grated Swiss cheese
½ cup cream
1 stick butter

In a large bowl, mix eggs and cream beat until well mixed. Slice the chanterelle mushrooms and in a large sauté pan place a tablespoon of butter. Allow melting, add the mushrooms, and cook until soft. Remove mushrooms to a paper plate, and discard the liquid.

Wipe out the sauté pan and reduce the heat on the burner. Using a stick of butter, wipe the bottom of the sauté pan and with a ladle or coffee cup dip out about ½ to ¾ cup of the eggs, pour into the pan on one half, sprinkle with Swiss cheese and add the cooked chanterelle mushrooms. Add lobster on top and allow to cook for about 2 minutes. Gently flip the uncovered side over on top and after about 1-2 minutes flip over. The omelet should be light and fluffy, not brown.

Eggs Benedict

Eggs (allow two per person)
Toppings (bacon, crab, bay shrimp, razor clams)
English muffins (one muffin per person)
Butter
3 Tbs. vinegar
Hollandaise sauce

Prepare your selected topping and set aside in a warm oven. Toast and butter the sliced English muffins and place into the oven to keep warm.

Pre-heat or prepare the hollandaise sauce. In a saucepan at least 3 inches high. Fill halfway full with water and add 3 Tbs. vinegar. Let the water come to a simmer, but do not let it boil. Add eggs making sure not to break the yolks. Poach eggs gently by shaking the pan a couple of times. Poach for 3-4 minutes and when ready remove with a slotted spoon.

To assemble: Place the two slices of English muffin onto plate, place a small amount of hollandaise sauce on top, add your topping and place the poached egg on top of muffins. Add more hollandaise sauce and serve.

Huevos Rancheros

8 eggs
1 large yellow onion
1 clove minced garlic
3 Tbs. olive oil
2 Tbs. flour
1 tsp. chili powder
½ tsp. oregano
Sea salt and pepper to taste
1-#2 ½ can of solid-packed tomatoes
½ lb. Jack cheese
1 small can green chili peppers

Chop onion and place into heated pan with olive oil and garlic. Cook until onions are clear and garlic is browned and add flour, chili powder and oregano salt and pepper to the pan. Add can of tomatoes and simmer for 10 minutes, then turn into a shallow casserole. Crack the eggs, being careful not to break the yolks. (You may want to break the eggs into a coffee cup and then slide them onto the casserole.) Slip a spoon under each one so they will each settle into their own little hollow. Arrange the eggs throughout the casserole. Place green chili peppers and cubes of Jack cheese amongst the eggs and put into an oven at 350 degrees until the eggs are set and the cheese is melted. Serve with tortillas and/or frijoles.

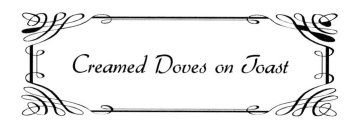

Creamed Doves on Toast

I used to make this for breakfast before school.

6 dove breast, deboned and cut in halves
1 cup milk
¼ cup . . . Flour
⅓ cup Marsala wine
Sourdough bread
Olive oil
1 Tbs. butter

Season breast with salt and pepper, roll in flour and fry in heated pan with olive oil. When browned, remove to a warm plate and add butter and flour to pan. Make rue, cooking until the flour is golden brown. Add Marsala wine and stir, add milk and season with salt and pepper to taste. Toast sourdough bread, place dove breast on top of the bread and cover with gravy and serve.

Clams on Toast

2 razor clams
2 slices sourdough bread
2 eggs

Bread clams and cook on high heat for 2-3 minutes. Fry the eggs until hard.

Toast the bread, butter it, and place the clams and eggs on the toast. Eat it like a sandwich. Yes, it's that simple and it is so good!

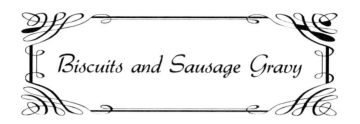

Biscuits and Sausage Gravy

1 lb. sausage
1 small yellow onion chopped
4 biscuits
2 Tbs. butter
3 Tbs. flour
1 cup cold water or if you want red eye gravy add cold coffee
2 cups milk

In a heavy cast iron pan, cook sausage. Once it is ¾ of the way done, add chopped onion and continue to cook until onions are soft and clear. With a slotted spoon, remove sausage and onion to a bowl and keep warm. Remove all the drippings from the pan, reserving it in a coffee cup. Do not scrape the pan. Add the flour to the cold water and mix into a thin paste. Add the butter to the pan along with 6 tablespoons of the sausage drippings (grease) mix and scrape the bottom of the pan to loosen up the good stuff. Slowly add the milk into the gravy and stir until thickened, add the sausage and onion back into the pan and adjust the seasoning with salt and pepper. Cut the biscuits in half and pour the sausage and gravy over the biscuits.

Dutch Baby

⅓ cup butter + 3 tablespoons
5 eggs
1 cup milk
1 cup flour
½ cup chopped pecans
2 apples peeled and chopped
¼ cup brown sugar
⅓ tsp. cinnamon

Put butter in a 9x13" baking dish and set in a 425 degree oven to melt. While butter is melting, put eggs in a blender and blend on high, slowly adding the milk until well blended, slowly add flour and blend for about 30 seconds. Remove the baking dish from the oven and pour the batter into the hot, melted butter. Return to oven and bake until puffy and nicely browned, about 20-25 minutes. While the Dutch baby is in the oven peel and chop up the apples in a heated frying pan. Add 3 tablespoons butter and brown sugar and heat until the brown sugar begins to caramelize. Add apples and pecans reduce heat, and allow to simmer. When the Dutch baby is done, remove from oven, pour the caramelized apples and pecans down the middle making sure to drizzle some onto the top and sides, sprinkle with a little powdered sugar, and serve with lemon slices and maple syrup.

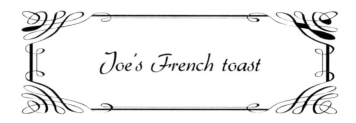

Joe's French toast

3 eggs
1 cup milk
½ tsp. orange extract
1 tsp. cinnamon
6 slices bread

In a large bowl beat the eggs and milk together, add the orange extract and cinnamon, and beat well until mixed. Heat up a pan and dip each slice of bread into the egg dip. Cook until brown on both sides.

Huckleberry Pancakes

3 cups flour
6 tsp. baking powder
3 tbs. sugar
1 tsp. salt
Sift the above ingredients together

1 egg
½ cup milk
¼ cup melted butter
1 tsp. vanilla
1 cup huckleberries

Mix together. Batter should have a few lumps in it; add more milk if it is too thick. On a hot greased griddle pour out batter to desired size of pancake, sprinkle berries on top of the pancakes. When bubbles appear in the pancakes, turn over and cook for about 1 minute more then serve.

Appetizers

Spring Rolls

1 lb. egg roll wrappers
1 lb. ground pork
1 lb. bean sprouts
1 cup shredded bamboo shoots
1 cup shredded carrots
2 cups cabbage shredded
4 green onions cut 1" long
4 cups oil to fry egg rolls in

Marinade for the pork

3 Tbs. soy sauce
1 clove garlic minced
½ tsp. sugar
2 tsp. cornstarch
1 tsp. sesame oil

Marinate the pork in a small bowl. While pork is marinating, wash and cut all of the vegetables and set aside. In a wok, heat 2 Tbs. sesame oil and add sliced green onions and pork and cook until pork is done. With a slotted spoon, remove pork and set aside, add all the vegetables, and cook until vegetables are done and most of the liquid is gone. Add pork back to the wok, stir to mix, and remove. Allow to cool.

In a small bowl add 2 Tbs. flour and 3 Tbs. cold water and mix into a paste. Lay out the egg roll wrapper and put about 3 Tbs. of the cooked filling on a corner of the wrapper and roll up the wrapper folding the opposite corners in towards the middle to form an envelope. Rub the flour paste on the edges and continue to roll. Repeat until finished and place egg rolls on a cookie sheet lined with parchment paper until ready to deep fry.

Heat 4 cups of oil to 375-400 degrees and deep-fry the rolls until brown and crisp. Keep warm in the oven, making sure to leave the oven door cracked open so they do not become soggy. Makes about 18-20 egg rolls.

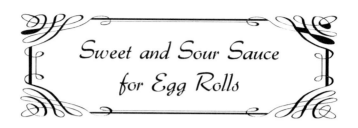

Sweet and Sour Sauce for Egg Rolls

4 Tbs. rice vinegar
4 Tbs. sugar
4 Tbs. ketchup
1 Tbs. cornstarch
½ cup chicken stock
½ cup water
A few drops of red or orange food coloring (optional)

Dissolve the cornstarch in water and add all the remaining ingredients. Bring to a boil until clear and thickened, remove and place in a bowl.

Three Rivers Spring Rolls

1 can of Spam
½ pound fresh green beans
½ pound carrots
1 package of egg roll wrappers
Ginger soy sauce for dipping
Enough oil to deep-fry

Rinse and trim the green beans, peel and trim the carrots, then cut and trim to the length and width of the green beans. Slice Spam length-wise and about the same thickness of the green beans. In a small bowl add 2 Tbs. flour and 3 tbs. cold water. Lay egg roll wrapper out and place 2 green beans, 2 carrot slices, and 2 slices of Spam. Fold the corner of the wrappers forming an envelope, rub the edges with the flour paste, and roll up. Repeat until finished. Heat 4 cups oil to 375-400 degrees and deep-fry the rolls until brown and crisp. Dip the rolls in ginger soy sauce and enjoy.

Ginger Soy Sauce

1 cup soy sauce
¼ cup brown sugar
1 tsp. minced fresh ginger
1 Tbsp. rice vinegar

Mix and allow to sit for at least five minutes.

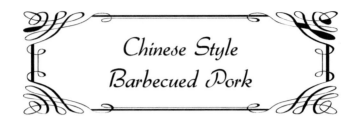

Chinese Style Barbecued Pork

2 lb. whole pork loin
1 green onion chopped
1 tsp. minced fresh ginger
2 cloves sliced garlic
2 Tbs. sweet rice wine
3 Tbs. soy sauce
2 Tbs. hoi-sin sauce
1 tsp. sesame oil
A few drops of red food coloring (optional)

Basting sauce

½ cup chicken stock
1 Tbs. honey
2 Tbs. soy sauce

Cut pork loin into two equal lengths so it will fit into a large 1 gallon Ziploc® bag. In a medium bowl add onion, ginger, garlic wine, soy sauce, hoi-sen sauce sesame oil, and red food coloring mix and pour into Ziploc® bag with the pork loins. Refrigerate and allow to marinate for at least 2 hours (overnight is better).

Pre-heat oven to 375 degrees. Place pork loins on a roasting rack and place in oven for 30 minutes. Turn once and bake the other side for another 30 minutes. Remove the loins from the oven and baste with the basting sauce brushing the sauce, on both sides and making sure to cover the sides and ends, Put back into the oven and bake for 10 more minutes, remove, turn and baste again and place back into oven for 10 more minutes, remove and allow to rest for 20 minutes before slicing. Can be served hot or cold with hot mustard sauce or Chinese Ketchup.

Mustard Sauce

2 Tbs. Coleman's dry mustard
1½ Tbs. cold water

Mix Coleman's dry mustard with cold water and stir until it becomes a paste. Add small amounts of water as needed. Let sit for five minutes before serving.

Chinese Ketchup

3 Tbs. ketchup
1 tsp. Worcestershire
A few drops of Tabasco sauce

Mix and allow to sit for five minutes

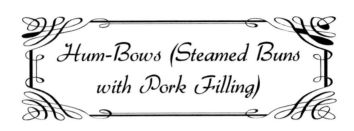

Hum-Bows (Steamed Buns with Pork Filling)

4 cups all-purpose flour
1 cup warm milk
2½ tsp. dried yeast mixed with 4 Tbs. lukewarm water
3½ Tbs. sugar
1 tsp. salt
½ tsp. baking soda

Mix dry yeast with 4 Tbs. lukewarm water and let it set for a couple of minutes. In large pan combine flour, sugar, salt and baking soda mix well and then form a well in the middle of the dry ingredients. Add milk and yeast mixture. Knead dough until all is mixed. Cover with dry towel and keep in a warm place and let it rise until double in size.

Filling

2 pounds diced or ground pork (bear meat is also really good in this recipe)
2 cups chopped bamboo shoots
1 ½ cup chopped yellow onion
4 tbs. soy sauce
1 Tbs. hoi-sen sauce
¼ tsp. cinnamon
Sea salt and pepper to taste
1 Tbs. sesame oil

Heat 1 Tbs. sesame oil in a wok and brown the onion and pork. Add the bamboo shoots and all the seasoning ingredients and simmer for about 10 minutes. If the cooked meat mixture is juicy, just blend 1 Tbs. cornstarch with 3 Tbs. cold water, and mix well and then add to the meat mixture, stirring until thickened. Place cooked meat into a strainer and let cool in the refrigerator for a couple hours.

Once the dough has doubled in size, knead the dough for about five minutes and roll into 16" long and 2" around. Cut in 1" pieces. On a lightly floured board, flatten each piece of the dough, and roll into 3" circular shape. Continue turning it clockwise to retain the round shape.

For each bun place a tablespoon of the filling on the dough. Gather the edge of the dough up around the filling in loose and natural folds. Bring the folds to the top of the ball and twist securely. Place buns on a lightly floured board and let rest for 10 minutes before steaming.

To steam, place a very wet paper towel in a steamer and set buns on about 1" apart. Steam for about 10-15 minutes. These buns can be frozen after steaming and reheated again by steaming.

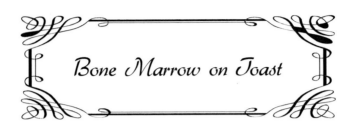

Bone Marrow on Toast

I cut elk and deer leg bones into 3" inch lengths, but you can also buy beef marrowbones at the store.

8-12 marrowbones
1 loaf of good bread (I like the Italian with garlic cloves)
1 lemon
Sea salt and course black pepper

Brown the bones by baking at 350 degrees until the marrow slips out easily. Mash it in a bowl, slice the bread and then slice the slices in half. Spread the marrow on the toast splash a little lemon juice on and season with salt and pepper.

Marinated Chanterelles

1 cup olive oil
1 pound fresh chanterelles dry, not waterlogged

Marinade

¼ cup balsamic vinegar
2 cloves sliced garlic
1 bay leaf
1 tsp. Dijon mustard
½ tsp. each fresh oregano, rosemary and basil
¼ tsp. sea salt

In a sauté pan heat the olive oil until it becomes very hot then add the chanterelles and toss them in the pan quickly for 3-5 minutes. Combine all the ingredients for the marinade, add the chanterelles and the oil from the pan to the marinade mix and refrigerate for at least 4 hours.

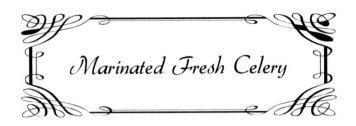

Marinated Fresh Celery

1 large bunch of fresh celery
2 quarts fresh cold water
2 tsp. anise oil or anise liquid flavoring

Cut and remove celery from the base, cut the leaves off and cut celery into 3" or 4" inch pieces. In a large bowl about 2-quart size add celery, water, and anise. Allow to sit in refrigerator for 4-5 hours. The celery will absorb the anise in this length of time and mix it with its own natural flavors. Remove the celery from the water and serve while chilled.

Salmon Lox

One salmon or steelhead fillet bones removed
⅓ cup tender quick curing salt
⅔ cup brown sugar
⅔ cup sugar
Fresh dill
⅓ cup Grand Mariner orange liqueur
1 fresh squeezed orange

You will need plastic wrap and a glass or plastic container large enough for the fillet to sit in. Remove pin bones from the fillet and place two pieces of plastic wrap in the bottom of the container in a cross pattern, making sure there is enough wrap to wrap the fillet in. Place the fillet skin side down.

Mix liqueur and orange juice together, paint the fillet and let it sit while you mix the salt and sugars together and then rub into the salmon fillet. Lay the fresh Dill on top of the fillet and then wrap fillet tight in plastic wrap and place in refrigerator for 4 days, turn once a day. On the fourth day remove from the plastic wrap and rinse in cold water.

The salt, sugar, liqueur and acid from the orange juice create a chemical reaction that cooks the fish, If you want to add a smoke flavor to the lox, run a pan of chips through your smoker and then without heat place the salmon lox into the cold smoker for about an hour and it will absorb the smoke flavor.

Smoked Fish Dip

½ pound salmon lox sliced thin
¼ pound smoked fish (sturgeon or salmon)
1 package cream cheese room temperature
¼ stick of butter
2 Tbs. heavy cream
1 Tbs. minced garlic
1 Tbs. minced onion (red or yellow)

Place cream cheese in a mixer and beat until smooth, add butter and cream and again beat until smooth. Add garlic, onion, and smoked fish and beat until mixed.

Line a small, rounded bowl with plastic wrap in a cross pattern, making sure it overlays the and completely lines the bowl. Take the sliced salmon lox and line the bowl overlaying the sliced lox. Once done, add the mixture of the smoked fish, cover the top with sliced lox, and cover with the plastic wrap. Let it sit overnight. When ready to serve, unwrap the plastic wrap, place a serving plate over the top of the bowl and turn over onto the plate. Carefully unwrap the rest of the plastic and adjust the salmon lox. Line the plate with sliced bagels and cut into 1" chunks or crackers.

Salmon Dip

1 tall can of salmon
1 8-ounce package of cream cheese
2 green onions chopped
1-2 tsp. Worcestershire sauce
1-2 drops of liquid smoke

Bring cream cheese to room temp. In a large bowl add all ingredients and mix well. Form into a ball and cover with plastic wrap. Allow to sit for at least an hour before serving. Best served after sitting overnight.

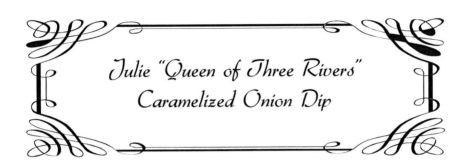

Julie "Queen of Three Rivers" Caramelized Onion Dip

2 large Walla Walla onions
¼ cup unsalted butter
¼ cup olive oil
¼ tsp. cayenne pepper
1 tsp. sea salt
½ tsp. black pepper
1 Tbs. balsamic vinegar
⅓ tsp. thyme
4 oz. cream cheese soft
½ cup sour cream
½ cup mayo

In a heated pan add butter and olive oil, then chopped onions, cayenne pepper sea salt, and black pepper. Cook until onions are browned and caramelized. Add balsamic vinegar and thyme, reduce heat, and cook for another 2 minutes. Remove from heat and allow to cool. In a large bowl place cream cheese, sour cream, and mayo, mix all together until smooth and then stir in the cooled onions with any juice from the pan. Mix well and allow to sit. This recipe can be made up to three days in advance.

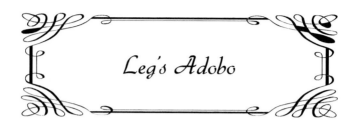

Leg's Adobo

25-30 assorted duck legs and thighs, skin intact (Grouse and pheasant
can also be used, or mix them all. Save the legs and thighs
throughout the season, freezing them until you have enough.)
2 cups pineapple juice
1 cup soy sauce
½ cup cider vinegar
1½ cups brown sugar
6 garlic cloves, sliced
1 Tbs. Tabasco sauce
2 tsp. chili flakes
1" fresh chopped ginger
4 green onions chopped
1 Tbs. course black pepper
2 Tbs. sesame seeds

Preheat oven to 450 degrees. In a large bowl combine the pineapple
juice, soy sauce, vinegar, brown sugar, garlic, Tabasco sauce, chili flakes,
ginger green onions, and pepper. Mix well and allow the brown sugar to
dissolve. Take a large baking pan and coat the inside with oil, add the legs
to the pan spreading them out, add the sauce, and cover the pan with foil
and place in the oven. Bake for 1 hour and then rearrange the legs in pan.
Cook for another hour and again rearrange the legs. After 2 hours, check
legs every 20 minutes, adding more liquid as needed. Cook until meat is
almost falling off the bones. Remove from pan, place on a serving tray,
sprinkle with sesame seeds, and allow to cool slightly before serving.

Oysters Wrapped In Bacon

1 pint fresh oysters (medium size)
Pepper bacon

Wrap oyster with half slice of bacon and secure with a toothpick. Once all the oysters are wrapped, place them on a cookie sheet and bake in the oven at 400 degrees for 10 minutes. Turn oysters over and bake for another 10 minutes. Or, place wrapped oysters on a heated grill and BBQ until bacon is crisp.

BBQ Oysters in the Shell

1 bushel of fresh bay oysters
½ pound grated Asiago cheese
1 pound melted salted butter
4 cloves chopped garlic
Hot sauce

Heat grill to high, melt butter, and add chopped garlic. Place shelled oysters on the grill and cover, and cook until shell opens. Be ready with gloves and a shelling knife. When shells open, remove the top shell, leaving the oyster in the bottom part, sprinkle with cheese and dash with melted butter, Worcestershire sauce, and hot sauce and eat it right out of the shell. Caution: there will be burnt fingers, but it is worth it!

Soups

Clam Chowder

1 pound frozen razor clams with juice, chopped
1 bottle Clam juice
¼ pound bacon
2-3 potatoes chopped
1 med. sweet yellow onion
4 stalks celery chopped
1 bay leaf
4-12 oz. cans of evaporated milk
1 pint of heavy cream

In a large stockpot cook bacon until crisp. Add onion, celery, and bay leaf and cook until the onions are clear. Add the clam juice to deglaze the pan, reduce heat, and add the evaporated milk and the chopped clams. Cook for another 3-4 minutes and slowly add the cream. Cook for another 5 minutes and season with salt and pepper and serve.

Crab Shell Bisk

Shells from at least 3 cleaned crabs
4 leeks
2 cloves garlic
Sea salt
½ pound crabmeat
1 Tbs. curry
1 lime zest and juice
1 can coconut milk
1 pint heavy cream

Place crab shells into a large stockpot and add enough water to cover. Cut the leeks, reserving the white, and add the green tops to the stockpot along with the garlic cloves. Bring to a boil and reduce heat and allow to cook for at least 2 hours. Strain and discard the shells. You should have about 4 cups of crab stock. To the crab stock add the juice and zest of the lime, chopped leeks, and coconut milk, season to taste with the sea salt and curry, reduce heat and slowly add the cream and the crabmeat. Serve immediately.

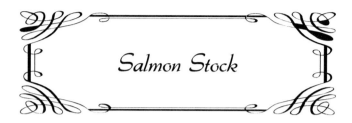

Salmon Stock

1 filleted salmon carcass with head attached
3 large leeks
Two whole heads of garlic
3 carrots
3 celery stocks
1 onion
¼ cup sea salt

In a large pot add all and cover with water. Bring to a boil then reduce heat and allow to cook until meat falls off the fish (at least 3 hours). Strain stock into a clean pot and discard the rest. Allow to cool, divide into 1 quart servings, and freeze.

Coconut Curry Salmon soup

4-6 cups salmon stock
1 pound fresh salmon skinned and boned cut into cubes
3 leeks white and the first part of the green chopped
2 celery stocks chopped
2 carrots chopped
2 potatoes cubed
1 can coconut milk
1 pint cream
2 tablespoons of curry

In a large pot add salmon stock, leeks, celery, carrots and potatoes. Cook until the potatoes are soft. Add salmon, coconut milk, cream and the curry; then bring the heat up but do not boil. Cook for about 5 minutes more and serve.

Salmon and Pumpkin Curry Soup

1 lb. salmon fillet, boned and skin removed, cut into about 1 inch chunks
1 can coconut milk
3 Tbs. curry
4 cups chicken stock
2 Tbs. fish sauce
2 Tbs. sugar
3 stalks of lemon grass
1 lime juiced
½ teaspoon turmeric
1 pound fresh pumpkin peeled and cut into bite-sized chunks
2 stalks celery diced
Salt and pepper to taste

In a large pot add everything except the salmon. Bring to a boil then reduce to a simmer. Cook until pumpkin starts to get soft but not mushy. Reduce heat and add salmon, cook for about 5-10 minutes more. Once salmon is added, refrain from stirring so as not to break it up.

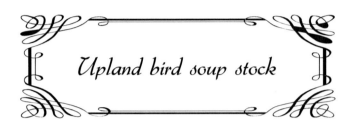

Upland bird soup stock

When I make my soup stock I use a twenty-quart pot and 12-20 bird carcasses. You can freeze the carcasses until the end of the season or until you have enough. Even one carcass will make soup stock you just have to adjust the rest of the ingredients. A rule of thumb is to use enough water to cover the carcass.

2-3 grouse carcasses
1 large onion
4 cloves garlic
2 whole carrots
2 stalks of celery
⅓ cup sea salt
2 Tbs. coarse black pepper

Place the carcasses in a large stockpot that is big enough to hold 4-5 quarts of water. Add the rest of the ingredients and cover with water, bring to a boil and reduce heat to simmer. Remove any scum that rises to the top and allow to cook for 2 hours and the liquid will cook down. Once you see that the bones are falling apart and what meat is left on them is falling off, remove the pot from the heat and pour into another stockpot. Using a strainer to capture everything but the liquid, discard the bones and vegetables. Let the stock cool and place into 1-quart bags and freeze.

Turkey Bean Broth/ Soup Stock Mexican Style

1 turkey carcass
1 sweet onion
6 cloves garlic
6 dried Mexican chilies
2 Tbs. cumin
3 Tbs. ground Oregano
3 Tbs. ground red hot chili powder
4-6 Tbs. sea salt
Water to cover

Place all in a large stockpot, cover with water, and bring to a boil. Reduce heat to low and simmer all day. Reduce stock to half then strain and freeze.

Thai Chicken Soup

2 Tbs. peanut oil
½ cup onion chopped
1 large carrot peeled and sliced on the diagonally
1 celery stalk sliced diagonally
2 cloves garlic minced
6 cups chicken broth
1 16-oz can coconut milk
¾ cup chunky style peanut butter
1 medium potato, diced
2 cups cooked chicken chopped
¼-½ teaspoon red pepper flakes

Heat oil in large saucepan over medium heat. Sauté onion, carrot, celery, and garlic until soft, but not brown. Remove from heat and stir in broth, coconut to a boil. Reduce heat and simmer until potatoes are tender (about 30 minutes).

Side Dishes and Sauces

One day back in the late sixties, dad was working in the barbershop when in walks my Uncle Dennis McCord with a couple of Canadian Officers. Now Uncle Denney was an officer in the USN and it was Rose Festival Fleet week in Portland Oregon. So Uncle Denney walks in and tells Dad that these fellow Naval Officers are in need of a good home cooked meal, and he had told them that Dad made the best Pasta in the world. Uncle Denny then asked dad if he could bring them over for Sunday dinner. Dad looked at the three of them and said, sure.

Now this was on a Monday. By Thursday the word had spread throughout both the Canadian and American fleets that there was going to be a big Italian party with all the home cooked pasta and wine you could handle.

You see my Uncle Denney and my dad kept inviting people. Now my Mom did not object to people coming over. The only question she had was how they were going to pay for it. So my dad and his pack of wild friends (The Italian Garden Society) got together had a couple of bottles of wine and came up with a plan.

They took a garbage truck, and decorated it with a bunch of balloons and ribbon's, got a couple of pretty young ladies attired in bikini's, then filled up a couple of clean garbage cans with booze and entered the Portland Merrykhana parade. They got the judges drunk and with a perfumed garbage truck, they won Grand Float honors for which they received a pretty ribbon and $50.00 bucks.

They took the money and paid for the party; On Sunday afternoon Uncle Denny shows up with One Hundred Naval officers and their girlfriends and the first Rigatoni Festival was under way. They won Grand float honors three years in a row. For the next 13 years, the Italian Garden Society had the Rigatoni festival for the Canadian and American officers in our backyard.

So in honor of the Italian Garden Society, I give you my dad's sauce that started it all.

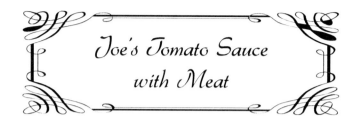

Joe's Tomato Sauce with Meat

4 pounds lean pork with all fat removed then ground
1 Tbs. black pepper
1 Tbs. salt
½ tsp. oregano
2 Tbs. fennel
¼ cup white wine or vermouth

Combine all of the above in a mixing bowl; mix with hands until ingredients are well blended.

In a very large, deep skillet, heat 3 Tbs. olive oil over medium heat. Crumble pork mixture into skillet sauté, browning it lightly, for 4 to 5 minutes, stirring often with a fork. Push meat to the side and add;

1 large onion, finely chopped
¾ cup celery finely chopped
1 medium green pepper, seeded, and deribbed and finely chopped
1 Tbs. fresh chopped garlic

Sauté until onions are transparent, adding more oil if necessary. Next add:

6-14 ½-ounce cans of Italian bell, Plum or pear tomatoes, coarsely chopped and including the juice from the cans
1 small can (6 ounce) tomato paste
1 Tbs. oregano
1 tsp. Thyme
1 tsp. basil

Stir into meat and vegetables, blending well; bring to a simmer over medium heat; reduce heat so that the mixture just barely moves and cook for 2 to 3 hours uncovered, adding a little warm water from time to time if the mixture seems too thick. Stir occasionally.

Cooked Fresh Tomato Sauce

12 ripe tomatoes
½ cup olive oil
1 small celery stalk with leaves chopped
1 medium onion chopped
2 garlic cloves chopped
2 Tbs. fresh basil chopped
1 Tbs. Fresh oregano chopped

Blanch the tomatoes by placing them into boiling water for a couple of minutes. After the skin begins to shrink, remove them from the water and run under cold water to finish the process of peeling. After the tomatoes are peeled, place them back into the pot with no water and bring to a boil until they are cooked (about 10 minutes). Mash them until they are the consistency of a cooked sauce. Heat the olive oil in a pan and add the celery, onion, garlic, and herbs. Cook until the onion is clear and the celery is tender. Add to the sauce, stir in, and allow to simmer. Water can be added to the sauce at this time if you want it a little thinner. Reduce heat and let simmer for at least 1 hour. Season with salt and pepper, add any herbs to taste, and if desired, add meat or fish and cook until they are cooked. This will make about 6 cups of sauce for about 1½ pounds of cooked pasta.

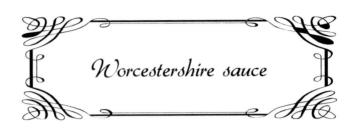

Worcestershire sauce

This stuff is awesome and is nothing like the Worcestershire you buy in the store. It is thick like catsup.

1 15-oz can of red kidney beans
1 6-oz bottle of soy sauce
1 tsp. garlic powder
2 salted anchovies or 2 sardines from a can
12-15 fresh apples peeled and sliced
2 gallons of apple cider vinegar (keep one gallon in reserve)
1 whole large onion sliced
3 Tbs. ground cloves
2 Tbs. ground turmeric
2 Tbs. ground nutmeg
3 Tbs. ground allspice
3 cups boiled black coffee

Second phase

2 tsp. red ground pepper
4 Tbs. cane syrup corn syrup can also be used
6 Tbs. salt
3 Tbs. yellow mustard
1 Tbs. sugar

In a large stockpot, add the first 12 ingredients. Only use one gallon of the vinegar and reserve the second gallon. Bring to a boil and slowly boil for 2 hours. As the water in the vinegar evaporates, add half water and half vinegar to replace it. Stir frequently, as apples burn easily and also tend to stick to the bottom of the pan. Remove from heat and allow to cool. Remove in batches and use a food processor to puree. Using the empty gallon vinegar jug, add 8 cups of the puree. To this, add the second phase of ingredients and remaining vinegar until the gallon jug is full. Place the cap on the container and shake it to mix all of the ingredients. Let stand for 24 hours before use. Store in the bottom of your refrigerator.

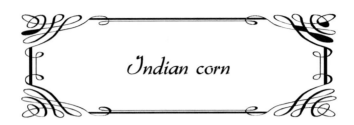

Indian corn

4 ears of corn shucked and the cornels cut off (1 corn cob per person)
¼ cup butter (½ stick)
1 Tbs. walnut oil
½ cup chopped walnuts

In a large skillet, set to medium-high heat and melt butter and add walnut oil. Add shucked corn and stir, cook for 10 minutes, season with sea salt and pepper, and serve.

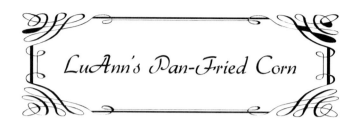

LuAnn's Pan-Fried Corn

4 ears of corn shucked and the kernels cut off
¼ stick butter
Sea salt
1 tsp. sugar

In a large skillet, heat butter and add corn sprinkle with sugar and cook for 10 minutes. Season to taste with sea salt and serve.

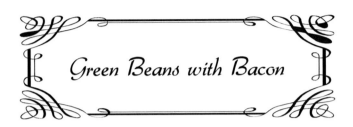

Green Beans with Bacon

1 lb. fresh or frozen green beans
¼ pound chopped bacon

In a large pot, place green beans and chopped bacon, cover with water, and bring to a gentle boil. Reduce and simmer for 45 minutes. Strain and serve.

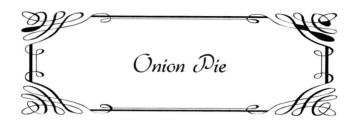

Onion Pie

6 strips of bacon
1 tsp. butter
½ cup heavy cream
1 cup grated cheddar cheese
6 sweet yellow onions sliced thin
2 eggs
1 Tbs. flour
1 tsp. salt
3 tsp. sugar
1 un-baked pie shell

Fry bacon until crisp then remove from pan. Pour off most of the grease and add sliced onions and butter. Sauté until onions are soft and clear. In a large bowl, add eggs and cream and beat until smooth. Add sugar, flour, and salt and mix, and then add the grated cheese. Place the pie shell in a deep-dish pie pan and poke the bottom with a fork. Add the onions, crumble the bacon and the remaining ingredients from the bowl mix gently, and bake at 400 degrees for 45 minutes or until golden and set.

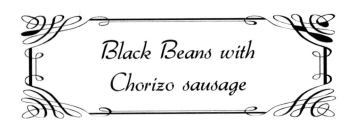

Black Beans with Chorizo sausage

½ lb. chorizo sausage, skin removed
2 cans black beans or 4 cups dried beans rehydrated
2 cloves garlic
½ yellow onion
1 tsp. ground cumin
1 tsp. dried basil
1 tsp. dried oregano
1 Tbs. olive oil
2 cups turkey bean broth

In a large cast iron skillet, add olive oil then chorizo and brown. Break it up in the pan and add garlic, onion, cumin, basil, and oregano. Cook until onion is soft and then add the turkey broth. Reduce heat and allow to simmer for at least two hours. Stirring just enough to keep the beans from burning, cook down until half the liquid is dissolved and serve.

Garlic Mashed Potatoes

6 Yukon potatoes peeled
6 cloves garlic peeled
1 tsp. sea salt
2 Tbs. butter
¼ cup heavy cream
Water to cover

Peel potatoes and cut into quarters and along with the garlic place into a pot cover with water and add salt. Bring to a boil and cook until a fork goes into the potatoes easily. Remove and drain water, reduce heat to low, and return pan to burner. Allow any remaining water in the pan to cook off, add butter and cream and slowly mash potatoes until desired texture. Some like it creamy and some like it chunky—who am I to judge?

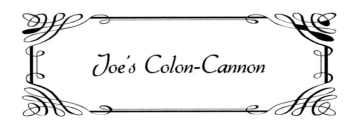

Joe's Colon-Cannon

This is an old Scottish dish called Colcannon. But if you find yourself cooped up in a small cabin or tent with a bunch of buddies you will see why I call it the Colon-Cannon.

2 medium-sized potatoes
2 large turnips
2 cups shredded boiled cabbage (about ½ head)
1 tsp. sea salt
1 tsp. coarse ground black pepper
1 cup milk
1 Tbs. butter

Shred the cabbage and boil in lightly salted water until soft. Drain and set aside. Peel and quarter potatoes and turnips and cook in lightly salted water. Drain well, turn burner off, and place pot back onto the burner. This will cook off the remaining water. Add butter and start mashing the potatoes and turnips while slowly adding the milk. Fold in the cabbage and add seasonings.

Succotash

2 cups fresh lima beans
2 cups fresh corn off the cob
1 tsp. salt
½ tsp. fresh ground pepper
3-4 Tbs. butter

Heat water to a boil then add corn, beans, and salt and pepper and cook for 10-12 minutes at a low boil until the beans are tender. Drain well, stir in butter and serve.

Zucchini Colistro

1 pound lean pork cut in thin strips
1 pound ground round of beef
¼ pound bacon, thinly sliced and cut into ½-inch strips
5 medium fresh zucchini
½ cup celery chopped
½ cup fresh Italian parsley
½ cup green peppers chopped
3 cups stale French bread or large course bread crumbs lightly toasted
3 eggs
1 tsp. salt
¼ pound fresh mozzarella cheese cut in ⅛ inch thick slices

Sauté pork and bacon in skillet over medium heat for 5 minutes. Meanwhile wash, the zucchini, and cut into 1-inch thick slices. Pour fat from skillet, add ground round, to the pork and bacon and cook for about five minutes, stirring often with a fork; then transfer to a large mixing bowl.

In the same skillet, sauté the celery, green peppers, and parsley for about 5 minutes, or until the celery is barely tender, adding olive oil if necessary and stirring occasionally with a fork. Add to the meat in the mixing bowl. Add zucchini to the same skillet, adding a little more olive oil if necessary, and cook until all pieces are heated through-about 5 to 8 minutes at most.

Meanwhile, add bread crumbs, salt and eggs to the mixture in the bowl and mix it with your hands until it is well mixed; to the pan with the zucchini add all of the ingredients from the mixing bowl, stir softly with a spatula and place all into a buttered shallow casserole dish; top with the sliced mozzarella cheese. Bake in a pre-heated oven at 350 degrees for thirty minutes.

Three Color Salad

10 oz. mozzarella cheese drained and sliced thinly
8 Plum or Romano tomatoes sliced
Sea salt and course black pepper
20 oz. fresh basil leaves
4 oz. extra virgin olive oil

Drizzle a little olive oil onto a serving platter. Arrange the tomatoes on a serving platter and season with sea salt and pepper. Lay a slice of mozzarella cheese on top of the tomato and a basil leaf on top of the cheese, Drizzle remaining olive oil on top and serve.

Fennel and Tomato Salad

1 bunch red leaf lettuce
6 medium fresh tomatoes, quartered
1 bunch fennel, thinly sliced
½ cup arugula, cut into small strips
1 dozen Sicilian dry-cured olives, pitted
6 Tbs. olive oil
2 Tbs. lemon juice
2 garlic cloves finely chopped
1 tsp. grated orange peel
¼ tsp. sea salt
Freshly ground pepper

Arrange lettuce leaves on a decorative platter and set aside. In a medium size bowl add quartered tomatoes, fennel, arugula and olives. In a small bowl add olive oil, lemon juice, garlic, orange peel, and salt and pepper. Mix well and adjust seasoning to taste. Pour over the tomato mixture and toss lightly. Add tomato mixture over the lettuce leaves on the platter and serve.

Sesame Spinach

1 lb. fresh spinach leaves
4 cups water
1 heaping tablespoon sea salt
2 Tbs. soy sauce
2 Tbs. sesame oil
¼ tsp. brown sugar
1 clove garlic finely chopped
1 heaping tsp. sesame seeds

In a large pot add water and sea salt, bring to a boil and add spinach leaves, cook until leaves start to turn color and become soft (about 5 minutes). Remove and drain well. In the meantime, add soy sauce, sesame oil, sugar, and garlic to a large bowl and mix well. Add cooked spinach and toss. Sprinkle sesame seeds on top and serve.

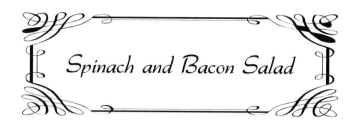

Spinach and Bacon Salad

1 ½ pounds fresh spinach
10 strips of bacon
4 Tbs. olive oil
6 Tbs. Balsamic vinegar
2 tsp. Herb mixture of (rosemary, tarragon, oregano)
2 tsp. Worcestershire sauce
2 tsp. Dijon mustard
4 tsp. sugar
Fresh ground pepper

Tear, wash, and dry the spinach and put into a salad bowl. Cut the bacon into 1-inch pieces and sauté until crisp. Drain off drippings, remove bacon, crumble, and mix into spinach. In the same pan mix olive oil, vinegar, herbs, Worcestershire sauce, mustard and sugar. Mix well and heat through. Add fresh ground pepper and pour over spinach. Cover bowl with a lid and let set for about 20 seconds. Toss the salad and serve.

Fresh Mushroom Soffritto

Olive oil
2 pounds fresh mushrooms (button or slice larger ones)
5 garlic cloves, chopped
3-4 small red hot peppers chopped
2 large sweet yellow onions
3 red bell peppers thinly sliced
3 green bell peppers thinly sliced
1 small can tomato paste
20 Sicilian dry-cured black olives pitted
2 Tbs. fresh oregano

In a large skillet, add enough olive oil to cover the bottom of the pan. Sauté the mushrooms, garlic, and hot peppers. Cook mushrooms until lightly browned and set aside on a platter. Add more oil if needed and sauté onions and peppers until tender. When peppers and onion mixture is slightly limp, add the cooked mushrooms. Sauté for a minute or so to blend all the flavors. Add 1 can of tomato paste and using a wooden spoon stir gently until the paste is dissolved and the vegetables are nicely coated with the sauce. Add oregano, pitted olives and additional salt and pepper if needed. Toss gently and simmer for about 1 more minute. Serve at room temperature.

Gnocchi Salad

1 lb. gnocchi, cooked and chilled
1 cup green peas, fresh or frozen
½ cup Sicilian dry-cured olives, pitted and halved
1 green bell pepper, seeded and chopped in bits
½ cup red onion, finely chopped
Pinch of dry mint or fresh mint, chopped

In a large bowl combine all ingredients and toss to mix. Set aside. In a small bowl add the following ingredients:
3 tbs. olive oil
2 tbs. red-wine vinegar
2 tbs. tomato paste

Mix and then pour over the salad and add salt and pepper to taste. Mix and refrigerate. Let sit for at least an hour and serve cold.

Morel Mushrooms with Couscous

¼-½ lb. fresh morel mushrooms
3 Tbs. chopped sundried tomatoes
3 Tbs. chopped sweet yellow onions
1 clove chopped garlic
5.8 oz. box of Couscous

Prepare couscous according to instructions, using chicken stock instead of water. In a separate pan, heat ⅓ cup chicken stock and add the cut mushrooms. Allow the liquid to escape from the mushrooms and reduce heat. Add onion and garlic and cook until the liquid is evaporated from the pan. Add the chopped tomatoes and couscous and stir. Adjust seasoning with sea salt and pepper and serve.

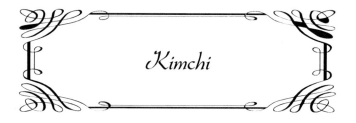

Kimchi

1 head Knappa cabbage
1 head Bok-Chow cabbage
1 cup salt
2 carrots shredded
4 cloves garlic chopped fine
5 green onion whites and greens (cut into 1" lengths)
1 Tbs. sesame oil
1 tsp. fish oil
4 Tbs. Chinese crushed red pepper
1 Tbs. beef consommé'
1 Tbs. sesame seeds

Rinse and chop Knappa cabbage and Bok-chow cabbage into about 1-2" inch pieces. Place into a large bowl and pour salt over cabbage. Mix to make sure all pieces are covered with salt. Cover bowl and let sit overnight. The next day, remove cabbage from the bowl and place into a colander; rinse with cold water. Rinse out the bowl and after rinsing the cabbage, taste one to determine if enough of the salt is out. It should be salty but not make your mouth pucker. Place the cabbage back into the bowl and add the shredded carrots, chopped green onions, garlic, Chinese red peppers, fish oil, sesame oil, and beef consume'.

Main Courses

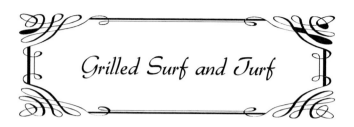

Grilled Surf and Turf

I learned this recipe in Perth, Australia—the Rock lobster capital of the world. One night, I ordered surf and turf; they brought out this big thick juicy steak and set it down in front of me. I looked at it and said, "That's a nice steak but where's the surf?" The waiter looked at me and said, "It's inside the turf, mate". So, I give you Grilled Surf and Turf.

2-3 lb. thick cut London broil sirloin steak (2-3" thick at minimum)
Optional substitute: backstrap or center cut pork loins (3" thick)
2 large tiger prawns per serving or 1 lobster tail per serving
Yoshida's Hawaiian sweet and sour sauce
1 garlic clove chopped and mashed
1 tsp. sea salt
Coarse black ground pepper

Cut a pocket in the center of the steak, making sure you do not cut all the way through. Mash the chopped crushed garlic with the sea salt and rub into the steaks. Peel the lobster tails or prawn tails and coat with sweet and sour sauce. Rub the inside pockets of the steaks and stuff with the tails then close the pocket with toothpicks. Cook on high heat over coals or a hot gas grill; sear both sides of steak 2-3 minutes per side. Remove from heat and let cook for 10-15 minutes more.

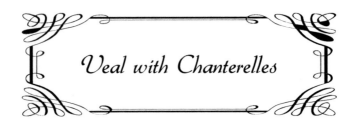

Veal with Chanterelles

8 veal scallops
4 Tbs. butter
3 Tbs. minced green onions
½ cup Marsala wine
⅔ cup beef broth
1 Tbs. cornstarch
¼ cup water
1½ cup cream
½ pound chanterelle mushrooms slice
Sea salt and coarse black ground pepper

Gently pound the veal until slightly flattened. In a sauté pan melt 2 tablespoons of butter and sauté the veal until both sides are brown.

Transfer to an ovenproof dish and place in a warm oven to keep warm. Add the onions to the pan and cook for about 1 minute. Pour the Marsala and beef broth into the pan and bring to a boil for about 5 minutes. Mix in the cornstarch with the ¼ cup of cold water and add to the pan along with the cream; cook until slightly thickened. In another pan add the remaining butter and sauté the chanterelles for about 5 minutes. Add to the sauce along with the veal and season with a little sea salt and fresh coarse pepper. Mix gently and serve with buttered noodles or rice.

Veal Marsala

6 Tbs. unsalted butter
6 2-oz veal scallops
Flour to coat veal
Salt and pepper to taste
2 shallots, chopped
3-4 ounces Marsala wine
6-8 fresh mushrooms thinly sliced
Parsley for garnish

In a sauté pan melt the butter over medium-high heat. Lightly dredge the veal with flour, shaking off any excess. Place the veal into the melted butter and lightly brown on one side. Sprinkle with salt and pepper, turn over, then slice, or plate. Add the Marsala wine to the pan and bring to a boil. Add the mushrooms and cook for about two minutes more to blend in the flavors. Pour the sauce over the veal and sprinkle with parsley.

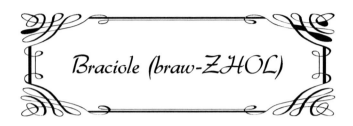

Braciole (braw-ZHOL)

1 ½ pounds beef round steak cut ½-inch thick in a single large slice or
    butterflied
1 ¼ cup bread crumbs
⅓ cup Italian parsley, finely chopped
6 large fresh mushrooms, finely chopped
⅓ cup freshly grated parmesan cheese
1 clove fresh garlic, finely chopped
3 eggs lightly beaten

Pound the round steak until it is less than ¼-inch thick. In a small
mixing bowl combine the bread crumbs and cheese, stirring well with a
fork. In a medium size bowl combine the parsley, garlic and mushrooms,
and stir these very well. Add the cheese and bread crumbs and stir until
well mixed. Add the eggs and mix until the mixture is smooth. Spread
on top of the round steak; roll it up and tie with butcher's string, tie on
both ends and once in the middle.

In transferring to the rack of a roasting pan, cradle the Braciole from
each end so as not to lose any of the stuffing.

Roast in a preheated, oven at 300-degrees for 1 ½ hours.

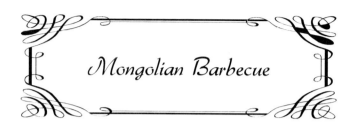

Mongolian Barbecue

1 pound flank steak
1 tsp. minced garlic and ginger oil
3 Tbs. chopped green onion

Seasoning ingredients for marinating beef

⅓ tsp. baking soda
2 Tbs. soy sauce
1 Tbs. cornstarch
¼ tsp. sugar
2 tsp. sesame oil
1 tsp. crushed hot pepper
3 cloves garlic sliced
4-5 slices' fresh ginger

Sauce

½ cup canned beef broth
2 tsp. Worcestershire sauce
½ tsp. vinegar
1 Tbs. ginger wine or rice wine
1½ tsp. cornstarch
2 tsp. soy sauce
1 clove garlic sliced
1 tsp. sliced fresh ginger

In a small saucepan on high heat, add 1 tsp. sesame oil, sliced garlic and ginger. Cook until the garlic turns golden brown then add remaining ingredients for the sauce. Stir constantly until thickened then remove from heat.

Slice flank steak against grain and cut into about 3 x 2 x ¼" thick pieces. Place seasoning ingredients in a bowl, add beef and mix thoroughly. Marinate for at least ½ hour.

In a wok heat 3 Tbs. sesame oil to high heat and add garlic and ginger. Add beef stir-fry until light brown and then add onion. Remove to a platter, pour the sauce over the cooked meat, and serve.

Canyon Classic Sticky Ribs

Gray Greenlee, one of my best friends, and I went over to the Deschutes River one night with a case of beer and a shrimp and pepperoni pizza. Little did we know at the time that this would turn into an epic event known as the Canyon Classic, Fishing Derby and Rim Rock Croquette tournament. At times there would be up to 50 people attending this. I don't remember the name of the guy who created the Sticky ribs, but I thank him.

1 rack of Pork ribs cut to single ribs
1 17-oz. bottle of Yoshida's Original Teriyaki sauce
1 bunch Cilantro
1 Tbs. chopped ginger
3 cloves garlic
3 Tbs. sesame oil
1 bunch green onions
Sesame seeds

In a wok heat the sesame oil, garlic and ginger until the garlic starts to turn color. Add ribs and brown. Add Yoshida's Original Teriyaki sauce, bring to a boil, and reduce heat. Cover and let simmer for 30 minutes. Remove cover and slightly increase heat until a gentle bubble is acquired; allow the sauce to reduce until it is a thick syrup consistency. Be sure to keep a close eye on it at this stage or it will become a blackened mess. Once the sauce is thickened, remove from heat, add cilantro and chopped green onions, toss and sprinkle with sesame seeds, and serve.

BBQ Chinese Ribs

5 lbs. short ribs, pork
Marinade
1 Tbs. rice wine
1 Tbs. rice vinegar
½ tsp. fish oil
¼ cup soy sauce
1 Tbs. honey
4 Tbs. Cane Syrup
2 Tbs. sesame oil
½ tsp. Chinese five spice
¼ tsp. baking soda
1 Tbs. cornstarch
1 Tbs. Chinese ground red pepper
1" fresh ginger sliced

In a medium sized bowl mix all ingredients (except ribs) until well blended. Rinse pork ribs and place into a large Ziploc® baggie, pour marinade over pork, and allow to marinate for at least 24 hours (2 days is ideal). BBQ over low coals for 30 minutes and enjoy.

Pulled Pork

4-5 pound shoulder pork roast with bone or Boston butt roast
Garlic powder
Salt and pepper

BBQ Sauce

1 14.5-oz. can stewed tomatoes and juice
2 cups water
1 cup cider vinegar
2 cloves garlic
2 bay leaves
1 sweet yellow onion
¾ cup brown sugar
1 tsp. sea salt
1 tsp. course pepper
1 tsp. New Mexico red chili powder
1 tsp. powder oregano
½ lemon with peel attached

Place all ingredients for the sauce into a pan and heat to a soft boil. Reduce heat and simmer for 1 hour. Remove lemon, making sure to squeeze out any juice back into the pan. Remove the bay leaves. Using a mixer, mix sauce until onion and tomatoes are puréed then turn heat to low and let simmer. Season the pork roast with salt, pepper and garlic. Turn grill or BBQ to high and sear all sides of the roast, about 10 minutes per side. In the meantime, heat oven to 200 degrees. Remove roast to a baking pan and pour the sauce over the roast. Cover with foil and place in the oven for 6-8 hours. Remove roast from oven and allow to sit for 10 minutes. Pull apart, put back into the sauce, and serve.

Baked Italian Sausage with Potato Wedges

6-9 Italian sausages
4 potatoes cut length wise into wedges
Large cast iron skillet
1 Tbs. olive oil
1 Tbs. fresh oregano chopped fine
1 Tbs. fresh Rosemary chopped fine
Sea salt

Cut potatoes into wedges and place into a bowl. Add olive oil and rub into the potatoes. Add oregano and rosemary and season with sea salt. Place the Italian sausages in a large cast iron skillet and work the potato wedges around the sausage and some on top of the sausage. Place into a preheated 400 degree oven. Bake for ¾ hour to 1 hour or until the potato wedges are golden brown and the juices run clear when the sausage is stuck with a fork.

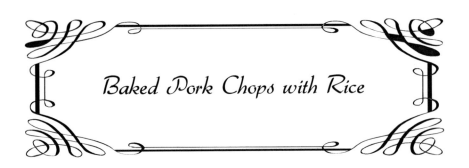

Baked Pork Chops with Rice

6 pork chops
1 onion chopped
1 clove garlic minced
Sea salt
Paprika
1 cup uncooked rice
1 can cream of mushroom soup
1 can beef broth

Preheat oven to 350 degrees. In a 9x13" baking dish add rice, onion, garlic, mushroom soup, and beef broth. Season pork chops with sea salt and paprika, place on top of the rice, and cover with foil. Bake in oven for 1½ hours and remove foil for last ½ hour of baking.

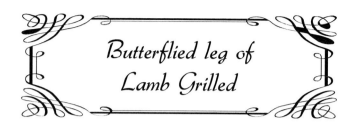

Butterflied leg of Lamb Grilled

When I was growing up my Grandpa had a farm in Yamhill, Oregon and he raised sheep. Grandpa Al's wonderful way with animals is another book just begging to be written. Anyway, I loved the spring lambs. Lamb is one of those meats that were created for the grill; the fat just bubbles and becomes crispy. Growing up, lamb was served two ways: with mint jelly and garlic or lemon and garlic.

6-7 pound leg of lamb, trimmed, boned, and butterflied
4 cloves garlic peeled and cut into small slivers
Sea salt and pepper
1 tsp. fresh chopped Rosemary
2 Tbs. butter

Trim the fat and debone the leg of lamb. (The butcher can do this as well when the lamb is purchased.) When the lamb is cut open, it should be approximately the same thickness all across—about 2½ to 3" thick. Spread out the lamb fat side down. Make tiny incisions in the meat with the point of a small sharp knife and insert the slivers of garlic, season the meat well with the sea salt, pepper, and rosemary.

Preheat the oven to broil. Lay the lamb on the oiled broiler rack with the fleshy side up, fat side down. Broil 6 inches from the heat for approximately 15-18 minutes, depending on the thickness. Brush the surface with melted butter, turn the lamb with tongs and broil fat side up for 16 minutes for rare or 20 minutes for medium rare meat. Test about 5 minutes before the end of the cooking time by removing the lamb form the broiler and inserting a meat thermometer in the thickest part—it should register 135 for rare or 140 for medium rare. When it reaches desired temperature remove it to a hot platter or carving board, fat side down and let stand for 5 minutes before carving. Carve slices crosswise on the diagonal.

Grilled Lamb Chops

The secret to a great lamb chop is to cook it rare to Medium rare in the middle and to have the fat on the outside crisp and slightly charred. Hot coals are required.

6 loin or rib chops at least 2-3" inches thick (at least 2 per person)
1 lemon
Cavender's All-purpose Greek Seasoning

Pre-heat coals until they are red-hot and turning white or turn your gas grill on high. Lay the chops out on a cutting board and rub the lemon juice into both sides of the chops. Season both sides with the Cavender's and place over hot coals. Cooking time will depend on the thickness of the chops and the intensity of the heat put out by the BBQ. For chops 2-4" inches thick, estimate a total cooking time of 9-12 minutes for rare and 12-14 minutes for medium rare. For chops 1-2" thick, estimate a total cooking time of 5-6 minutes for rare and 6-8 minutes for medium rare.

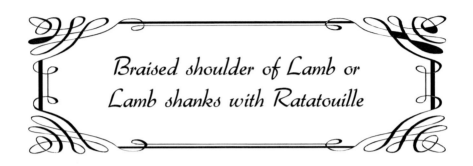

Braised shoulder of Lamb or Lamb shanks with Ratatouille

4-5 pound shoulder of lamb boned and tied or 5-6 lamb shanks
6 cloves of garlic peeled and cut into slivers
2-3 anchovy fillets cut into small pieces
Salt and freshly ground black pepper
Olive oil
2 medium onions, thinly sliced
4 small zucchini, trimmed and cut into ½ slices
1 green pepper, halved, seeded and cut into thin strips
1 medium eggplant peeled and diced.
2 Tbs. fresh basil chopped
2 ½ cups canned Italian plum tomatoes
¾ cup pitted, soft black olives
¼ cup plus 2 tbs. chopped fresh parsley

Make small incisions in the meat with the point of a small sharp knife and insert half the slivered garlic, (reserving the rest for later) and add the anchovy pieces into the incisions. Rub the meat well with salt, pepper, and olive oil and put it on a rack in a roasting pan. Roast for 30 minutes in a 400-degree oven.

While the meat is roasting, make the Ratatouille. In an 8-quart braising pan heat 5 Tbs. olive oil and add reserved garlic, zucchini, and green pepper. Sauté over medium-high heat for 5 minutes then add the eggplant. Mix the vegetables well with a wooden spatula. Season with 2 tsp. salt, 1 tsp. pepper, and basil.

Remove the lamb from the oven and place it in the middle of the vegetable mixture in the braising pan. Add the tomatoes and bring the mixture to a boil on top of the stove. Reduce the oven heat to 325 degrees and braise the lamb in the oven. Cover for 1½ to 2 hours or until the lamb is tender and the ratatouille is cooked down and well blended. Add olives and ¼ cup parsley and cook for 10 minutes longer. Transfer the lamb to a hot platter and remove the strings. (If lamb shanks were used instead of shoulder of lamb, place one lamb shank per person onto serving plates.) If the ratatouille is too watery turn the heat to high and reduce it down, making sure it does not stick to the bottom of the pan. The consistency should be thick. Slice the meat and serve with the ratatouille spooned over and around it. Sprinkle with chopped parsley and serve with crisp hot French bread.

Cabbage Rolls

1 head cabbage
1 lb. Jimmy Dean's country sausage
1 lb. lean ground beef
2 slices rye bread
2 cups V-8 juice or other tomato juice
1 yellow onion chopped fine.
2 Tbs. cilantro
1 egg
1 cup beef broth
Sea salt, pepper to taste
Fresh ground nutmeg to taste

Remove the outer leaves from the cabbage, core the cabbage with a paring knife, and submerge whole head in boiling salty water. Simmer for 10-15 minutes. As the leaves become tender, break them off and then plunge into ice water. Cut out all the heavy ribs and dry the cabbage between pieces of paper towel.

Cut the crest from the bread and place into a large bowl with 1 cup of V-8 juice. Add sausage, hamburger, onion, cilantro, egg, sea salt, pepper and a little ground nutmeg and mix by hand.

Lay out the cabbage leaves (overlapping the leaves). Put 4-5 ounces of meat mixture in each cabbage leaf. Fold the leaf over the meat and roll it. Repeat until all of the meat mixture is gone.

Line a casserole dish with sliced onions, carrots, and celery. Place cabbage rolls on top and brush with a little olive oil. Add the remaining cup of V-8 and the beef broth. Cover with foil and bake in a 325-degree oven for about 90 minutes. Remove the rolls and cook the sauce for another 15-20 minutes to reduce and pour over the cabbage rolls.

Wild Game

Wild game can be used for almost every recipe in this cookbook. When I refer to venison; deer, elk, moose, antelope, caribou, and sheep are the game animals that can be used. Bear meat can be used for any recipe calling for the use of pork. Cougar and Bobcat are very good eating. The meat is clear and white, tender and delicate and not gamey at all.

Grouse, quail, chucker, Huns, pheasants, partridge, and rabbit can be used for any recipe calling for the use of chicken. Ducks and geese are a little different. It is important to note that there is a difference in how to prepared wild ducks and geese compared to farm raised. Domestic ducks and geese are fatter and fed a steady diet, while the wild ones fly a long distance and eat some strange stuff along the way. The wild ducks and geese taste a little different, but they are still good eating.

Next to cooking, hunting and fishing have been one of my favorite life's pleasures. I could write an entire book on just wild game and fish (and maybe someday I will) but for this book I will just include some of my favorite recipes.

Remember that wild game will need to be handled and cooked differently. When in the field, always be sure to gut the animal quickly, get it cooled down, and keep it dry. Never overcook venison or duck. When cooking with venison, be sure to have everything prepared and ready to serve before the venison is cooked. Once the venison is ready, it should be plated and served immediately. When I'm lucky enough to harvest a bear I treat it just like pork. Hang it in a cooler at 32-38 degrees for no more than one or 2 days before you butcher it. I remove most of the fat and render it down for lard.

Grilled Backstrap Wrapped in Bacon with Huckleberry Reduction Sauce

4 1" thick steaks cut from the backstrap
4 thick slices of bacon (apple wood or pepper work well)

Huckleberry reduction sauce

2 cups fresh huckleberries or 1 pint of huckleberry jam
1 cup Chicken stock
1 cup red wine

In a small sauce pan place huckleberries if fresh add about 2 cups of water and one tablespoon of sugar. Cook until the berries burst then reduce heat and cook until half of the liquid is reduced. If using jam, add about ¼ cup water and again cook until reduced by half. Add chicken stock and cook until reduced by half. Add wine and again cook until reduced by half then turn down to a simmer and keep warm.

For the steaks, lightly season with a little salt, pepper and garlic powder, wrap with bacon and secure with a toothpick. Have grill preheated and place steaks on grill, cook about 4-5 minutes per side then with tongs pick up and roll the steaks in order to get a good crisp on the bacon. Steaks should be medium at this point; remove and plate. Drizzle the huckleberry reduction sauce over the steaks then serve and enjoy.

Whole Grilled Backstrap with Tomato Gravy

1-2 lbs. backstrap
Sea salt
Coarse ground pepper
Garlic powder
1 can Ramona tomatoes cut in sauce with basil
2 Tbs. olive oil
2 medium leeks cut
1 yellow bell pepper
½ lb. button mushrooms whole
¼ lb. Sicilian olives

In a large skillet add olive oil, mushrooms, bell pepper, leeks and olives and cook until the mushrooms start to release their juice. Add the can of tomato sauce then reduce heat and allow to simmer

Preheat grill to high, season backstrap with salt, pepper and garlic powder, place backstrap on grill and sear for about 3 minutes. Turn backstrap a quarter turn on the grill and cook for another 3 minutes then turn over and repeat. The backstrap should be medium rare. In the meantime, the sauce should be reduced down and thickened at this point. Place half of the sauce on a platter, remove backstrap, and allow to sit for 3-4 minutes. Slice backstrap against the grain and reassemble on top of the tomato gravy. Drizzle remaining gravy over the top and serve.

Venison Steaks with Spinach, Mushrooms, and Blue Cheese

4 venison steaks cut 1" thick.
1 lb. mushrooms sliced
1 bunch of whole leaf spinach cut in thirds
1-2 cloves garlic sliced thin
1 medium sweet onion cut in half and sliced
¼ cup red wine
½ tsp. beef consume'
Blue cheese
1 Tbs. butter
3 Tbs. olive oil

In a large cast iron skillet, heat olive oil and butter to medium-high heat, season steaks with a little sea salt and cracked pepper and add garlic slices and steaks to the pan. Sear steaks on both sides, about 2-3 minutes a side and remove the steaks to a platter. Add onions, mushrooms, wine, and beef consume' and cook for about 5 minutes until the mushrooms start to go soft. Place steaks back into the pan and add spinach and cook until spinach is done. Remove all except the juice to a hot plate, turn heat to high and cook down the sauce until it is slightly thickened (there should only be about 3-5 tablespoons left in the pan). Plate the steaks and cover with the mushrooms, onions, and spinach, top with the crumbled blue cheese and then drizzle the pan sauces over each serving and enjoy.

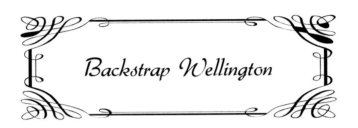

Backstrap Wellington

1½ to 2 lbs. whole backstrap deer or elk with fat trimmed
Sea salt
Coarse ground pepper
Garlic powder
1 Tbs. butter
3-4 green onions finely chopped
1 clove garlic finely chopped
6-7 mushrooms finely chopped
1-2 Tbs. Madeira wine,
⅓ cup stuffing
½ cup apple cider
1 sheet frozen puff pastry, thawed

Rub the backstrap with the salt, pepper and garlic powder, heat 1 tablespoon of olive oil and the butter in a medium-high pan and sear all surfaces of the meat, including the ends (about 6-10 minutes). Remove the meat from the pan and set aside to cool.

Add onions, garlic cloves, mushrooms, breadcrumbs, and apple cider. Sauté for about 3-5 minutes, cooking down the apple cider. Remove from heat.

In a food processor, add the stuffing mixture and blend until smooth, it should not be watery. Roll out the puff pastry on a floured surface until it is big enough to wrap around the backstrap. In the center of the pastry spread some of the stuffing and place the backstrap on top. Cover the top and sides of the backstrap with the remaining stuffing and moisten the edges of the pastry with the egg wash. Wrap the pastry around the backstrap (overlapping the edges to form a seam) and pinch lightly to seal. Place the wrapped backstrap onto a greased baking sheet so it is seam side down. Brush with the egg wash and bake at 350 degrees for 15-20 minutes. Serve and enjoy.

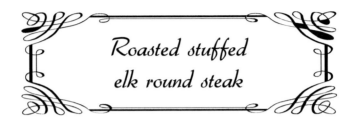

Roasted stuffed elk round steak

1 large elk round steak (beef or buffalo work well also)
3 cups dry breadcrumbs or stuffing
6 chanterelle mushrooms chopped (or any mushroom picked or purchased)
¼ sweet onion chopped
2 sticks celery chopped
1 Asian pear peeled and chopped
1 egg
1 cup chicken stock

Pound the round steak to flatten it out a bit, lightly season with sea salt and cracked pepper and set it aside.

In a large mixing bowl add stuffing, onion, celery, and pear. Add egg and mix by hand. Slowly add the chicken stock until the stuffing starts to break down and bind together (don't allow to wet). Once the stuffing is mixed, spread it onto the round steak about ¼" to no more than 1" thick. Roll the round steak up like a jellyroll and stick two large wooden skewers through it. Place it seam side down in a shallow oiled pan, cover with foil, and place in the oven at 425 degrees for 30-35 minutes. Remove foil and bake for another 10 minutes. This should come out to about medium to medium-well (adjust your cook time for rare).

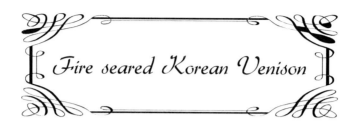

Fire seared Korean Venison

1 lbs. venison

10 green onions

2 Tbs. soy sauce

1 Tbs. rice wine

1 Tbs. sesame oil

1 tsp. sugar

2 garlic cloves peeled, crushed and chopped fine

1 Tbs. fresh finely chopped ginger

1 Tbs. sesame seeds

1 Tbs. crushed red peppers

½ tsp. baking soda

Slice venison into thin strips, and place into a bowl. In a separate bowl mix the soy sauce, rice wine, sesame oil, sugar, garlic, ginger, sesame seeds, red peppers, and baking soda. Pour mixture onto venison, cover and allow to marinade for at least an hour. Take a cast iron skillet or a wok and place on top of a burner set to high; keep it there until it is white hot. While skillet is heating cut the green onions into 1inch sections and set aside. **"Now for the fun part"** take 3 Tbs. sesame oil *CATION **the oil will flame up when it hits the skillet.* Just as the flames start to die down add the venison and marinade, quickly stir fry until all is browned about 2-3 minutes, add the green onions cook until onions are softened and serve.

Hot and Spicy Kung Pao Kitty

2 lbs. Cougar or Bob Cat backstrap sliced and diced
1 lb. fresh Chanterelle mushrooms
¼ cup cashews or peanuts
10 whole red hot peppers
3 cloves garlic

Marinade for the cat meat

1 Tbs. dark soy sauce
1½ Tbs. ginger wine
1½ Tbsp. Cornstarch
½ tsp. sugar
¼ tsp. baking soda

Slice and dice the kitty and place in the marinade. Allow to sit for at least 30 minutes or more. In a heated wok, add 3 tablespoons sesame oil and sauté red hot peppers, peanuts, and garlic. Stir in the marinated kitty and sauté for 3-4 minutes or until the kitty changes color. Add the chanterelle mushrooms and continue to stir-fry until the mushrooms are heated through. Splash with soy sauce and sesame oil and serve.

Bobcat Casserole

2 lbs. bobcat or cougar meat
½ cup butter
1 tsp. chopped fresh thyme
1 tsp. chopped fresh rosemary
1 tsp., chopped fresh parsley
½ cup chicken bouillon
½ cup white wine
Sea salt
Pepper

Remove all fat from the cat meat. Slice ¼ inch thick and lightly season with salt and pepper. Heat butter in skillet and brown meat on both sides. Transfer to casserole dish. Combine thyme, rosemary, parsley with the chicken broth and wine. Pour over meat, cover casserole, and bake at 350 degrees for about 45 minutes.

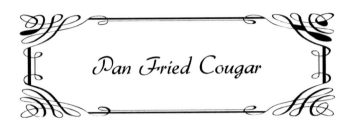

Pan Fried Cougar

1 lb. cougar backstrap
Salt
Pepper
Garlic powder
Chili powder
Butter
Olive oil

Slice cat meat about ¼ inch thick and season both sides with salt, pepper, garlic powder, and chili powder. In a heavy cast iron skillet heat olive oil and add butter. In small batches add seasoned cat meat and brown on both sides (about 2-3 minutes per side). Remove to paper towels and serve.

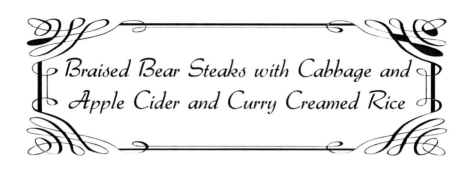

Braised Bear Steaks with Cabbage and Apple Cider and Curry Creamed Rice

4-6 bear steaks about ½-1" inch thick (pork steaks can be substituted)
Small head or ½ head of large cabbage
2-4 cups apple cider
Sea salt and pepper to taste
Olive oil
1 cup uncooked rice
3 cloves garlic sliced
1½ cup chicken stock
1 cup heavy cream
2-3 Tbs. curry
½ tsp. coriander
½ tsp. paprika
1 lb. chanterelle mushrooms
2 heavy skillets

Take one of the heavy skillets—add just enough olive oil to cover the bottom and heat it on high. Salt and pepper the steaks and add to the pan, searing on both sides until they are nice and brown. Add apple cider until it comes up about half way on the steaks and reduce heat to medium. Cut the cabbage like you would for coleslaw, add to the pan, and cover and let simmer for about 20 minutes.

In the second skillet, add olive oil again just to coat the bottom. On medium-high heat add uncooked rice and sliced garlic, cook until garlic and rice are just turning brown. Add chicken stock, mushrooms, curry, coriander, and paprika, stir and reduce heat and cover with lid or foil. Let simmer for about 20-25 minutes.

Remove steaks and cabbage from the first skillet, keeping as much juice in the pan as you can. (I try to arrange the cabbage on the serving platter and then place the steaks on top of the cabbage.) Place in a warm oven. Turn the heat up on the pan and reduce the apple cider, stirring to keep it from burning. Reduce it down until it is a thick syrup consistency, remove the steaks from the oven and pour over the steaks.

Remove the cover from the second skillet and check rice for doneness—it should be tender—if not, let simmer a bit longer. When rice is tender, slowly add cream until the rice is creamy but not soupy. Give it a stir and then serve with the steaks. The combination of flavors is amazing. Enjoy!

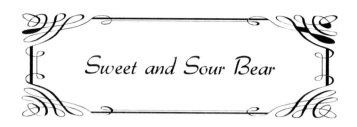

Sweet and Sour Bear

2 lbs. bear meat or pork

Marinade

1 egg yoke
1 tsp. sesame oil
4 Tbs. soy sauce
2 Tbs. cornstarch
1 Tbs. fresh ginger chopped fine
2 cloves garlic sliced

Sweet and sour sauce

4 Tbs. ketchup
2 Tbs. corn starch
¼ cup sugar
1 cup chicken stock
¼ cup rice vinegar
1 can fresh or canned pineapple
1 red bell pepper and 1 yellow bell pepper cut into chunks
1 small yellow onion cut up into chunks
Optional: a few drops of red food coloring

Trim all fat off the meat and cube into 1" pieces. Add to marinade and let sit for at least 1 hour before cooking.

For the sweet and sour sauce, add the first 5 ingredients to a pan and heat until it boils. Reduce heat and add peppers, onions and pineapple. Taste and adjust seasonings to taste. Set aside.

Using a wok or deep fryer, add about four cups of oil, peanut or canola. While oil is heating take a one-gallon Ziploc® bag and add one cup of cornstarch. Remove marinated meat from the refrigerator and in small batches add to the cornstarch and shake until all the pieces are coated with cornstarch. Place the meat into the heated oil (deep fry in small batches so your oil stays hot). Cook until golden brown and done. Pre-heat oven to 300 degrees, place the cooked meat into a large metal colander, and place it on a cookie sheet. Put the colander of meat on the cookie sheet in the oven. Make sure to keep the oven door slightly open—this will keep the meat crisp and hot. When all of the meat is cooked, plate and cover with sweet and sour sauce.

Bear-N-Beans

1 lb. bear meat cut in 1" cubes or stew cut
4 cloves garlic
1 yellow onion
1 Ancho pepper
1 lb. dry red beans
1 Tbs. sea salt
2 Tbs. ground cumin
1 tsp. ground course pepper
1 gallon beef stock
1 small can of tomato sauce (about 2 cups)
1 can chopped tomatoes

Soak beans overnight in fresh water. The next day rinse and place beans and bear meat into a crock-pot. Chop up garlic, onion, and pepper and add to crock pot. Add beef stock and remaining spices, cover with the lid, and cook all day on low. You may need to add more liquid throughout the day. Cook for at least six hours, the longer the better. This is not a chili—it is a bean dish that can stand on its own or be served as a side dish with a good steak.

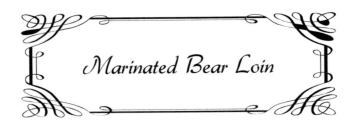

Marinated Bear Loin

1 whole bear loin, 6-7 lbs. (pork loin can also be used)
3 Tbs. vegetable oil

Marinade

2 medium sweet yellow onions chopped
1 bunch green onions chopped
4 carrots chopped
3 ribs celery chopped
¾ cup vinegar
2 tsp. sea salt
4 cups red wine
3 cloves garlic minced
1 tsp. coarse black pepper
4 bay leaves
2 tsp. fresh chopped tarragon or ½ tsp. dry

Sauce

½ tsp. minced garlic
1 tsp. minced pickled onions
1 tsp. chopped capers
2 tsp. chopped green onions

1 Tbs. fresh chopped parsley
1 cup sliced mushrooms (Morals are killer in this, but store bought will do)
¾ tsp. sea salt
¼ tsp. coarse black pepper
3 Tbs. butter
3 Tbs. flour
1 clove crushed

Remove any sinews and fat from the bear loin. Put all of the ingredients for the marinade into a large saucepan and bring to a boil and cook for about 5 minutes covered. Let cool.

Place the loin into a crock or large ceramic bowl—any non-metallic container will do. Keep in a cool place for 4 days, turning the meat over daily. When ready to cook, remove the meat, reserving the marinade, and wipe dry. Cut the loin into about ¾-1" chops. In a heavy cast iron pan heat 2 tablespoons olive oil and 1 tablespoon butter then brown the meat (about 2-3 minutes per side). Only cook a few pieces at a time (do not crowd the pan), removing the browned pieces and adding more oil if needed. Continue until all of the chops are browned. Place in a warm oven.

To prepare the sauce, add the garlic, pickled onions, capers, green onions, parsley, mushrooms, salt, and pepper into a food processor and puree into a paste. Strain 2 cups of the reserved marinade into it and blend.

Melt the butter in the skillet, stir in flour, and cook slowly until it is a nice brown color (a rue). Add the crushed clove and take the pan off the heat. Stir in the sauce then return to the heat and stir until thickened. Add the browned chops and slowly simmer for about 10 minutes over low heat, stirring frequently to ensure the bottom doesn't burn. The sauce should be thick and very flavorful. Serve with garlic mashed potatoes.

Stuffed Heart

1 deer or elk heart
1 box Stove Top cornbread stuffing
2 sweet Italian sausages
1 apple
1 small yellow onion

Soak the heart in salt water overnight. When ready to cook, trim and hollow heart, reserving any meat trimmed out. Remove Italian sausage from casings and brown along with any of the reserved meat. Dice up apple and onion and add to the stuffing along with the sausage and heart meat. Stuff the mixture into the heart and place into a baking dish. Place excess stuffing around heart and bake at 365 degrees for an hour and serve.

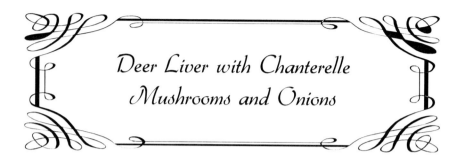

Deer Liver with Chanterelle Mushrooms and Onions

1 deer or elk liver
4 Tbs. bacon grease (or enough oil to coat the bottom of a cast iron pan)
1 cup Pride of the West seasoned flour
1-2 lbs. chanterelle mushrooms sliced
1 packet Lipton onion soup mix
2 large sweet onions halved and sliced
¼ cup milk
2 shots of whiskey

Trim liver of all fat, slice into ¼" slices, and soak in milk for at least 30 minutes. Place Pride of the West seasoned flour into a large Ziploc® bag, add sliced liver, and shake to coat. Season with a little cracked pepper. Heat a large cast iron skillet with three tablespoons of oil or enough to cover the bottom of the skillet. Cook liver in small batches, browning on both sides until done (oil may need to be added to the pan while cooking). Place liver in a warm oven until all of it is cooked. Once cooked, add sliced mushrooms and onions to the same pan. Once the water starts to extract from the mushrooms, add the Lipton onion soup mix and stir until mixed in. Add the whiskey and light the vapors with a lighter (be careful when doing this—a large blue flame will appear over the pan). When the flame starts to reduce, mix the contents and reduce heat. Let simmer until onions are soft and mushrooms are cooked. Water may need to be added, but do not do so until ready to serve. Remove onions and mushrooms, plate liver and cover with onions and mushrooms. In a container, mix 2 tablespoons of flour with about ⅓ cup cold water and add to the juices in the pan, turn heat up and scrape the pan mix all parts. Season to taste and pour over the liver, onions and mushrooms.

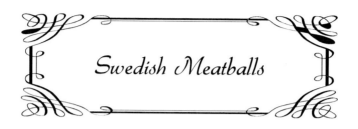

Swedish Meatballs

2 lbs. ground meat (venison, beef, or buffalo)
1 lbs. ground pork
1 tsp. sea salt
2 eggs
½ cup rolled oats
½ cup minced onions
½ tsp. coarse black pepper
2 Tbs. milk
2 Tbs. chopped cilantro
Grated lemon peel from one lemon and juice
½ tsp. nutmeg
2 packages brown gravy mix
1 cup red wine

In a large bowl, add everything except the gravy mix and red wine and mix by hand. Remove about 1 teaspoon of mixture and in a small pan heat and taste—adjust seasonings if necessary. Cover bowl and let sit overnight.

The next day, shape into balls about the size of walnuts. In a large fry pan, add a small amount of oil and fry meat balls a few at a time until they are well browned. Remove from fry pan and place into a crock-pot. When all of the meat balls have been browned, add 1 cup of red wine to the heated pan, scrape all the good stuff off of the bottom of the pan, then add the gravy packets along with 3 cups of water. Heat the pan; once the gravy starts to thicken pour over the meatballs and let simmer in the crock-pot for about an hour. Can be served as a main dish over cooked noodles or as an appetizer.

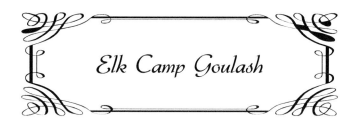

Elk Camp Goulash

Goulash is one of those dishes that is just good eating. This will feed about 10 normal people or 6 wet, cold, hungry hunters. The recipe can be downsized to accommodate smaller servings and not all of the ingredients need to be added.

6 lbs. of meat in the following order
2 lbs. beef chuck cut into 1" cubes
2 lbs. lamb shoulder steaks debone and cut into 1" cubes
2 lbs. boneless pork roast cut into 1" cubes
¼ cup olive oil
2 yellow onions chopped
½ head cabbage chopped
1 Anaheim pepper seeded and chopped
1 Serrano pepper seeded and chopped
5 cloves of garlic chopped fine
¼ cup tomato paste or 1 small can
2 cans stewed tomatoes juice and all
2 tablespoons whole caraway seeds
1 Tbs. sweet paprika
½ teaspoon marjoram
1 tsp. thyme
¼ cup balsamic vinegar
2 1-gallon cans beef broth

2 cups red wine
4 cups uncooked Mac noodles
2 bay leaves

In a large cast iron skillet add olive oil and brown meat in small batches until brown. Remove and place into a large stockpot. When all of the meat is cooked, deglaze the pan with a small amount of the wine, then add onions and cook until they caramelize. Add garlic, cook a few minutes more, and then add to the meat. Add remaining ingredients and stir. Cover and let simmer for about 1 hour or until the noodles are soft.

Moose Stroganoff

2 lbs. moose round steak (or any other type of meat)
4 Tbs. Worcestershire sauce
1 onion cut into chunks
2-3 cloves garlic sliced thin
1 can mushroom soup
1 can beef broth
1 cup red wine
4 Tbs. olive oil
Sea salt to taste
2 cups sliced mushrooms
Egg noodles

Slice the meat into thin strips and place into a bowl. Add the Worcestershire sauce and let sit for at least 30 minutes. In a large cast iron skillet or Dutch oven add enough olive oil to cover the bottom of the pan and then add about 2 tablespoons more oil. Heat until the oil starts to smoke, then add moose meat and juice from the bowl. Cook until brown then add onion, garlic, and mushrooms and continue to cook until onion is soft. Add beef broth, mushroom soup, and wine. Reduce heat to low and allow to simmer. In a large pot add 4 cups water, 1 tablespoon of olive oil, and 1 tablespoon of sea salt. Bring to a boil and add egg noodles, cook until noodles are done, remove noodles from water and drain. Add egg noodles to the stroganoff and stir until the noodles absorb most of the sauce and serve.

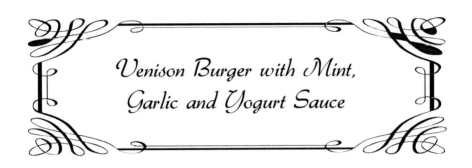

Venison Burger with Mint, Garlic and Yogurt Sauce

This is a Greek dish normally served with ground lamb.

2 lbs. venison burger
1 medium yellow onion chopped
4 cloves of garlic (2 chopped and 2 sliced)
2 cups chopped fresh mint leafs
2 cups Greek plain yogurt
¼ cup chopped roasted red peppers
¼ teaspoon crushed chili peppers
¼ cup pine nuts

In a medium bowl add yogurt, 1 cup of the fresh chopped mint, 2 chopped cloves of garlic, crushed chili peppers, and roasted red peppers. Mix and set aside.

Pour 2 tablespoons of olive oil in a heated skillet and heat the onions and remaining sliced garlic. Cook until the onions are clear. Add the pine nuts and cook for about 3-5 minutes then remove from pan and add to the yogurt sauce.

In the same pan, add half of the venison and cook until brown (about 5-8 minutes) then add the remaining venison and cook until done (some of the venison should be crispy). Add the remaining cup of mint and remove from heat. Add to the yogurt sauce and serve with Pita bread or over spaghetti noodles.

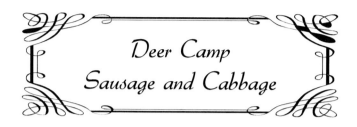

Deer Camp Sausage and Cabbage

2 lbs. sausage sliced ¼-1" thick (Kielbasa, Beer Brats, etc. can be substituted)
1 head cabbage
1 sweet onion
2 cloves garlic
2 Tbs. butter
1 can stewed tomatoes
1 11.5-oz. can of V8 juice

Cut cabbage into chunks about 1x1" and place into hot skillet. Add onions and cook until soft then add sausage, stewed tomatoes, v8, salt and pepper to taste, and add hot sauce if you like it kicked up. Cover and cook down until sauces reduce by half and serve.

Venison Chile Verde

2 lbs. of venison (the tougher cuts like the flank or rump roast)
2 cloves of garlic sliced
Ground cumin
Sea salt
Ground oregano
1 sweet onion cut in half and then sliced
1 Poblano pepper seeded and sliced length wise
1 Ancho pepper seeded and sliced length wise
1 jalapeño pepper seeded and sliced length wise
3 cups Chile salsa
1 cup of uncooked rice
1 can pinto beans drained

Pound the venison steaks until slightly flattened and season both sides with sea salt, cumin, and oregano. In a large cast iron skillet heat until oil starts to smoke, add meat and sear both sides quickly (cook only a few steaks at a time so you do not lose the heat from your pan). Remove the cooked meat and place on a platter. When all of the meat is cooked, reduce heat, add the onion, garlic, and peppers and cook until they just start to become soft. Remove from pan and add uncooked rice along with the 3 cups of salsa and 1 cup of water. Slice meat into strips and add back to the pan. Reduce heat and simmer for about 35 minutes or until rice is done. Add the pinto beans, onions, and chilies back into the pan and stir until the beans are heated through. Serve on heated burrito shells with sour cream.

Chile Salsa

12 fresh tomatoes peeled and chopped
6 cloves of garlic chopped
2 large sweet yellow onions
4 Ancho Chile peppers
4 Poblano Chile peppers
3 jalapeño peppers
3 gypsy peppers
8 tomatillos
¼ cup fresh chopped cilantro
6 tablespoons ground cumin
3 Tbs. sea salt
1 lime

Grill the onions and peppers. Remove skins and seeds from peppers, coarse chop, and place into a large stockpot. Add the chopped tomatoes and the rest of the ingredients and cook over medium heat for about 20-30 minutes. Season to taste, allow to cool, and serve.

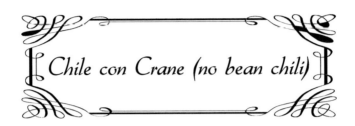

Chile con Crane (no bean chili)

2 lbs. of meat, venison, beef or bear

2 lbs. of pork (boneless ribs work well for this dish)

4 cloves of garlic chopped up fine

1 Tbs. bear lard or olive oil

3 bay leaves

1 quart ripe tomatoes diced (juice and all)

1 large yellow onion chopped

6 Tbs. New Mexico Chile powder mixed with one 1 tablespoon of flour

2 Tbs. ground oregano

2 Tbs. ground cumin

1 Tbs. sea salt

Cut meat into cubes about half inch square. In a large Dutch oven or stockpot with a lid, melt the bear lard or olive oil. Dice the onion and garlic and brown them in the oil. Add the meat and 3 level tablespoons of water; cover and steam well for about 5 minutes then add the tomatoes and juice. Mix the Chile powder with the flour. Add enough cold water to make a thin paste then add to the pot. Now add the oregano, cumin, and salt and cook slowly for about 2 hours. If needed, add water to keep from burning.

Red Bear Chili

2-3 lbs. bear shoulder roast deboned (or pork shoulder roast deboned)
Powdered oregano
Powdered cumin
Sea salt
2 cups Hearty Red wine
7 cloves garlic peeled
1 onion cut in half
4 dried Pasilla-Ancho chilies (stems and seeds removed)
4 dried New Mexico red chilies (stems and seeds removed)
4 cups water
1 8-oz. can tomato sauce
1 14.5-oz. can stewed tomatoes

Season both sides of the roast with sea salt, oregano, and cumin and rub into the roast. In a heated Dutch oven add 1 tablespoon olive oil, sear the roast on both sides, and toss in the garlic cloves, onion, and chili peppers. Add wine and water (enough to cover the roast) and cover with a lid. Reduce heat and simmer for at least 2 hours or until the roast can easily be pulled apart by hand or with forks. When ready, remove the roast to a cutting board and allow to cool. With a slotted spoon remove the chilies, garlic, and onion and place into a blender. Strain off the oil from the broth and add 1 cup of broth and canned tomatoes to the blender. Blend on high to form a sauce, slowly add more broth to desired thickness (usually about 1 more cup will do). Taste and adjust the seasoning if necessary. Remove any broth left in the Dutch oven and set aside. The roast should be cool enough to handle at this point—pull the meat apart and place back into the Dutch oven. Add the can of stewed tomatoes and the chili sauce, stir, and reheat. Serve with Tortilla shells or with Spanish rice.

I have harvested my fair share of deer, elk, Moose, caribou, and bear. But I have harvested thousands of rabbits and squirrels and I have to say I really love rabbit. The following recipes can be used with rabbit, squirrels, muskrat or birds.

Chicken Fried Rabbit with Cream Gravy

2 cottontail rabbits cut into serving pieces
4 Tbs. flour
Salt and fresh ground pepper
5 Tbs. lard
2 Tbs. flour
¾ cup milk
½ cup heavy cream

Shake the rabbit in a paper bag with flour, salt, and pepper. In a large cast iron skillet with a lid, melt the lard until hot then turn heat to medium. Cook until all sides of the rabbit are golden brown. As the rabbit browns, it will absorb enough fat to require more lard; add as needed. When all the meat is brown, turn heat to low, cover, and simmer for about 12 minutes. Turn the pieces a couple of times during this process. Turn heat to medium, remove lid, and turn the pieces to allow moisture to evaporate. Remove rabbit to a hot platter, pour off all but 3 tablespoons or so of fat, stir the flour into the fat and dredging and cook over low heat until the flour is brown. Remove skillet from heat and stir in the milk, then place back on low heat and cook until it starts to thicken. Stir in the cream and continue to heat but do not boil. Serve with fresh biscuits or mashed potatoes.

Roast Rabbit

This can be cooked over an open fire, rotisserie or on a flat grill. The cooking time will remain the same.

1-2 cottontail rabbits skinned and left whole
Sea salt
Black pepper
Garlic powder
Stuffing for rabbit
4 cups bread crumbs
2 eggs
Cream
Butter
Herbs
Parsley
Sweet marjoram
Thyme
Nutmeg
Sautéed onion and celery

Place breadcrumbs in a large bowl. Melt butter and sauté the onions and celery until onions are clear. Add to the bread crumbs then add eggs and enough cream and herbs and mix until bread is moist. Season to taste with herbs. Season the rabbits inside and out with the salt, pepper, and garlic powder. Stuff with the stuffing and sew or truss up the rabbits. Cook for about 1½ hours, basting often with lard or butter. For a really crisp brown crust, alternately baste with cold lard or butter and dust with flour while the spit is turning.

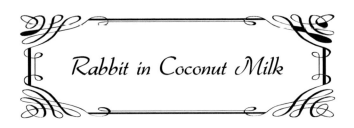

Rabbit in Coconut Milk

2 cottontail rabbits cut into serving pieces
6 cloves garlic
1 tsp. sea salt
¼ tsp. cayenne pepper
½ tsp. cumin
Freshly ground pepper
3 Tbs. cider vinegar
1½ Tbs. oil
1 Tbs. sweet paprika
1 sweet yellow onion chopped
1 large tomato, peeled, seeded, and chopped
1 Tbs. tomato paste
½ cup thick coconut milk

Mash the garlic with the salt, cayenne, cumin, and a dozen turns or so of the pepper grinder. Stir in the vinegar. Spread this mixture over the pieces of rabbit in a large Dutch oven. Cover and let marinate for about 4 hours, turning the pieces once or twice.

In a small pan heat the oil and paprika then add the onion and cook until the onion is soft. Add to the marinated rabbit then add the chopped tomato, tomato paste, and enough water to barely cover and bring to a boil. Cover and cook over low heat until the rabbit is tender (about 1½ hours). Lift out the rabbit with a slotted spoon to a serving dish and keep warm. Reduce the liquid over medium-high heat to about 1 cup, stirring frequently. Turn heat to low, stir in the coconut milk, and heat through (but don't let it boil). Pour over the rabbit and serve.

Upland Birds, Chickens, and Ducks

I love hunting upland birds, and a finer eating bird is hard to come by. The bones of grouse, pheasants, quail, chucker, doves, pigeons and wild turkeys make the best soup stock you could ever ask for and boy do the legs and thighs make for great chicken and dumplings. It is for this reason that I divide the upland bird into four sections: breast, legs, and thighs, then the carcass with the heart, liver and giblets included. I love hunting with people who think the breast is the only thing worthwhile on a bird. They always are happy to give me the carcass, at least until they see what I can do with it.

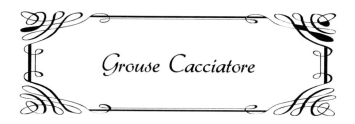

Grouse Cacciatore

In Italian, cacciatore means "hunter style". This recipe is adapted from the chicken cacciatore my dad used to make. Chicken or pheasants go quite well with this recipe, but for me there is nothing better than grouse and no place better to serve it than in deer camp the night before the deer season opens.

6 grouse breasts
1 large sweet yellow onion
2 green bell peppers
2 pounds fresh mushrooms (chanterelle are ideal for this dish)
1 can chicken broth
1 cup Marsala wine
1 cup of flour
⅓ cup seasoned olive oil
Seasoned roasted red peppers and garlic (recipe to follow)

Dredge grouse breast in flour and season with salt and pepper. In a large skillet (or Dutch oven) pour some of the seasoned olive oil from the roasted peppers into the pan and brown the grouse breast (about three to four minutes a side). Add green peppers, onion, and chanterelle mushrooms then cook about 3-4 minutes more. Add chicken stock and Marsala wine along with the red peppers and some of the garlic from the seasoned oil. Reduce heat, cover, and let simmer for about 30 minutes.

Seasoned Olive Oil with Roasted Red Peppers

Roast about a dozen red bell peppers that have been cut in half and seeded. Peel the skins and place them in a large quart mason jar. Add a dozen cloves of garlic that has been peeled, four whole stems of fresh basil, oregano, and rosemary. Fill with olive oil, seal with a lid, and let sit for about two days before using.

Marmalade Chicken

1 whole chicken cut into serving pieces
½ cup butter
¼ cup olive oil
1 can chicken broth
1 jar of marmalade jam
¼ cup brown sugar
¼ cup brown mustard
1 cup flour
1 tsp. sea salt
1 tsp. pepper

Season the flour with salt and pepper and place into a large Ziploc® bag. Place cut up chicken into the bag and shake until all of the chicken is coated. In a large cast iron skillet with high sides, heat butter and olive oil. Add chicken and brown on all sides. Add chicken broth and cover, then reduce heat to low and cook for about 35-40 minutes. In a small pan add marmalade jam, mustard, and brown sugar and bring to a boil. Remove chicken to a baking dish and pour marmalade sauce over the chicken, coating all sides. Place into a preheated 350-degree oven and bake for 25 minutes. Turn chicken over, add more glaze, and bake for another 25 minutes.

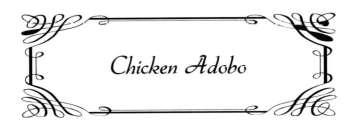

Chicken Adobo

1 whole chicken cut into serving pieces
1 cup flour
¾ cup vegetable oil
2 Tbs. sesame oil
3 Tbs. cornstarch
1 cup brown sugar
1 cup chicken broth Chilled
1 cup rice vinegar
⅓ cup soy sauce
2 cups fresh pineapple cut into chunks

Cut chicken into serving pieces and rub with sesame oil. Put the cut up chicken and flour in a large Ziploc® bag and shake until chicken is coated. In a large skillet heat oil and brown chicken. Place the chicken into a 9x13" baking dish in a single layer. In a mixing bowl add brown sugar, cornstarch, vinegar, soy sauce, and cold chicken broth. Mix until the cornstarch and brown sugar is dissolved. Add the pineapple then pour over the chicken. Bake in a preheated oven at 350 degrees for 1 hour (turn chicken over half way through cooking time). Serve with rice.

Curried Chicken

1 whole chicken cut up into serving pieces
Sea salt
Paprika
1 Tbs. butter
1-2 Tbs. curry powder (red or yellow)
1 large apple (or 2 small ones) peeled and chopped
1 yellow onion chopped
1 can cream of mushroom soup
1 cup heavy cream

Season cut up chicken with sea salt and paprika and place into a buttered 9x13" baking dish in a single layer. In a heated skillet add butter and sauté the onion and apples. Sauté until the onions are clear, add the curry powder, cream of mushroom soup, and the cream then heat for about 2 minutes. Taste and adjust by adding more curry or more cream. Pour over chicken and bake at 350 degrees for 1½ hours.

Sesame Chicken with Garlic Sauce

1 whole chicken boned and cut into one inch pieces
1 egg yolk
2 Tbs. soy sauce
⅛ tsp. garlic powder
4 cups oil (for deep fry)

Garlic sauce

1 Tbs. sesame oil
5 cloves garlic minced
1 tsp. minced fresh ginger
½ cup chicken stock
1 Tbs. sugar
¼ tsp. ground pepper
2 Tbs. soy sauce
2-3 chopped green onions
1 Tbs. sesame seeds

Batter

1 cup + 2 Tbs. flour
¾ cup cold water
3 Tbs. cornstarch
2 eggs beaten
2 tsp. sesame oil
2 heaping tsp. baking powder
1 Tbs. sesame seeds

Bone and cut up the chicken then marinate with the egg yolk, soy sauce, and garlic powder for about a ½ hour to 1 hour. Prepare the batter and mix until smooth. Dip the marinated chicken into the batter and deep-fry until golden brown. Fry a few pieces at a time to avoid dropping the temp of the oil. Drain off the oil and place chicken in a warm oven. Be sure to leave the oven door slightly open or the chicken will become soggy.

In a wok heat sesame oil and sauté garlic and ginger until limp. Add chicken stock, sugar, soy sauce, ground pepper and bring to a boil until the sauce becomes a little thick (about 5 minutes). This should make about a ⅓ of a cup or less. Pour over chicken, add sliced green onions and sesame seeds, and serve right away.

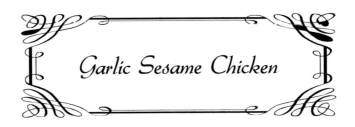

Garlic Sesame Chicken

4 cloves garlic sliced
½ tsp. fresh grated ginger
2 Tbs. sesame oil
2 Tbs. sweet rice wine
1 Tbs. rice vinegar
½ cup soy sauce
¼ cup brown sugar
1 tsp. baking soda
3 dry red chilies
2 Tbs. fresh cilantro chopped fine
1 whole chicken cut into serving pieces
1-2 Tbs. sesame seeds
3 green onions cut in half lengthwise

Combine first ten ingredients in a glass bowl and mix to create the marinade. Cut the chicken into serving pieces and place into a large 1 gallon Ziploc® bag, stir marinade, and pour it into the bag. Allow to marinate for at least 4 hours (overnight is better).

Preheat oven to 350 degrees, place chicken skin down into a 9x13" casserole dish and pour marinade over the chicken. Place in oven and cook for 1½ hour's. After 45 minutes turn chicken over and continue cooking until nice and brown. Remove from oven and plate. Sprinkle with sesame seeds and cut green onions.

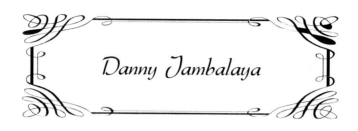

Danny Jambalaya

When my daughter Madilyn turned 14 years old, I asked her what she wanted for her birthday dinner. Madilyn looked down at the bird pen and said, "I want to shoot Danny the rooster and eat him". At the time we were raising chickens, pheasants, chucker, ducks, turkeys, and quail. Danny (who we had raised from a chick) was 3 years old and being the only rooster, was the king of the roost. Every day, Madilyn would go down and feed the birds. Carrying her metal pail with grain, Danny always took it upon himself to make sure he was the first one fed or he would attack her. Madilyn would face the attack and calmly swing the bucket like she was delivering a slow-pitch softball, smack Danny across the yard and then proceed to feed the birds. Danny would shake it off and go about feeding, waiting for Madilyn to turn her back so he could attack again. Yes, I think it is safe to say that Madilyn and Danny hated each other. So with a tear of pride in my eye, I loaded up Madilyn's six shot .22 with birdshot and walked her down to the bird pen.

The gun battle that took place was epic. It was high noon; Madilyn checks her pistol, squares her shoulders and begins her walk to the bird pen. I began humming the theme song from a Clint Eastwood Western—you know the one. Madilyn enters the pen, dust swirling around her booted feet; the birds stop and freeze, looking at her, realizing something is not right. Danny steps to the door of the birdhouse, looks at Madilyn, and their eyes lock. Madilyn is poised in the classic gun fighter's stance. Danny lifts his head and roars, "Cock-a-doodle-doo" and charges for the doorway, flying at Madilyn, razor sharp spurs and beak held out in front like daggers, ready to tear Madilyn apart. In one smooth motion, Madilyn raised the pistol and shot Danny right in the head in full flight. Danny crumpled in the dust. I swear to God, the rest of the birds cheered. To the victor go the spoils. I give you Danny Jambalaya.

1 whole chicken
1 lb. shrimp deveined and shelled
1 lb. smoked sausage
1 large yellow onion chopped
5 cloves garlic (3 whole, 2 minced)
1 cup chopped celery
1 cut up red bell pepper
1 cut up Poblano pepper seeds removed
1 can chopped tomatoes with juice
2 quarts of water
1 tsp. fresh chopped basil
1 bay leaf
2 tsp. hot pepper sauce
1 tsp. ground cumin
1 tsp. cayenne pepper
6 Tbs. sea salt
3 cups uncooked rice
½ cup chopped green onion
½ cup tomato sauce

In a large stockpot add chicken and 2 quarts of water; make sure the bird is covered. Add chopped basil, bay leaf, ground cumin, and sea salt. Cook for about 1½ hours (the bird should be cooked but not falling off the bone). Remove chicken from the water, reserving the broth. Once the chicken is cool enough to handle, remove skin and bones, placing the meat into a large bowl. Remove some of the fat from the chicken stock in the pan and add the chopped onions, chopped peppers, canned tomatoes, celery, and hot pepper sauce. Allow to simmer for 5 minutes.

Taste and adjust seasoning as needed. Add uncooked rice and reduce to a simmer. Add chicken, smoked sausage, shrimp, and tomato sauce. Stir and simmer for about 1-2 hours, adding a little water if needed to keep rice from sticking to the bottom. Add chopped green onion and parsley just before serving.

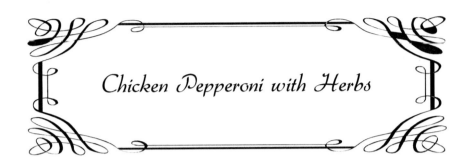

Chicken Pepperoni with Herbs

1 whole chicken
Sliced pepperoni
Fresh Fennel * the green tops
Fresh rosemary
Fresh basil
Fresh oregano
2 cloves garlic

Pre-heat oven to 325 degrees Rinse chicken, starting at the top of the chest cavity gently start working your fingers under the skin until it is lose but still intact, you want to make a pocket between the meat and the skin. Once this is completed start placing the sliced pepperoni under the skin making sure to work it down onto the thighs and legs. Rub the outside of the chicken with olive oil and season lightly with salt and pepper. Make a bundle of the fresh herbs and place into the cavity of the chicken along with the garlic cloves. Place into oven and roast at 325 for 20-25 minutes per pound or until the juices run clear. * The leftover bones, herbs and pan juices make an awesome soup broth

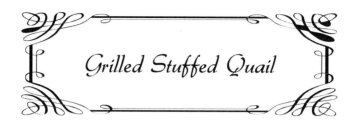

Grilled Stuffed Quail

Quail (2 per person)
1 slice of bacon per quail
Enough grapes to stuff the birds

Fill the quail with 8-10 squeezed fresh grapes (retain the grape juice for basting). Wrap the quail with a slice of peppered bacon and secure with a toothpick then broil or barbecue, turning often to keep the bacon from burning, baste with the squeezed grape juice.

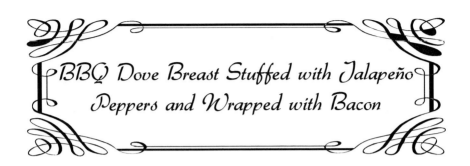

BBQ Dove Breast Stuffed with Jalapeño Peppers and Wrapped with Bacon

I have used quail and pigeons for this recipe as well.

Dove breast (about 3 per person)
Jalapeño peppers with top and seeds removed
Bacon
Rudy's BBQ sauce or mesquite BBQ sauce (you can order Rudy's BBQ sauce online or head on over to Texas and get some)

Season the breast with salt, pepper and garlic powder. Take the cleaned jalapeño pepper and place it in the back of the breast. Wrap with bacon and secure with a toothpick. Place on the BBQ and cook until the bacon is crisp. Baste with the BBQ Sauce and move to the side of the grill, away from the coals. (If you have a gas grill, turn one side off and close the lid.) Cool for another 10 minutes and serve. This goes really well with grilled corn on the cob and red beans and rice.

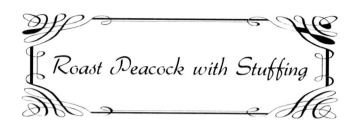

Roast Peacock with Stuffing

We had not lived in Battle Ground, Washington long when one of our neighbors moved away. Before they left, they turned all of their damn birds lose—several of which were Peacocks. Now there is no arguing that Peacocks are beautiful birds, until it's 4:00 am in the morning and they are screaming. One day, three Peacocks walked up onto our back deck and I decided it was time to introduce them to my lab, Trooper. The Peacocks flew up to the top of my house and then two of them flew down into the lower field. I turned Trooper loose and when they saw him running they flew off. The third one was a little late flying off of the house and he flew down to where the other two were. So two birds are flying away while one bird is flying in and Trooper was running at full speed. The bird landed right in front of Trooper and he plowed into the bird. Both went tumbling and Trooper came up holding the Peacock by the neck and fetched him in. I broke the neck and then had a 15-pound Peacock, which I cleaned and plucked. While stuffing the Peacock the next day, I hear a noise at the kitchen window, and low and behold the other two Peacocks are watching me stuff their buddy. I swear it's true. You can't make this stuff up . . .

1 5-10 lb. whole cleaned peacock, plucked and skin attached
Breaded Stuffing * I use a cornbread stuffing

Rinse bird inside and out and season with salt, pepper, and garlic powder. Prepare stuffing and stuff (similar to a turkey). Place into a roasting pan; add a cup of water, cover with a foil tent, and bake at 325 degrees for about 15-20 minutes per pound (basting often). Remove and let sit for 10 minutes before carving. Make gravy with the pan drippings just like a turkey dinner. The Peacock will taste a lot like pheasant.

Roast Goose Wrapped in Bacon

1 whole goose skinned
2 apples peeled and diced
1 medium yellow onion
2 stalks of celery
1 egg
½ lb. sweet Italian sausage
6 slices pepper bacon
1 bag stuffing (cornbread or sourdough)

Place stuffing into a large bowl. Chop apples, onion, and celery and add to the stuffing. Remove casings from sausage. Place 2 tablespoons of butter in a heated skillet and add sausage. Cook the sausage in the butter until cooked then add all to the stuffing mix. Add egg and enough water to moisten the stuffing. Rinse goose and season with sea salt and pepper, stuff goose with the stuffing, and wrap with the pepper bacon. Place in the oven at 350 degrees for about 1½ hours (Extra stuffing can be placed in a casserole dish and baked alongside the goose.)

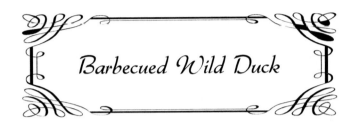

Barbecued Wild Duck

1 cup olive oil
½ cup red wine vinegar
¼ cup soy sauce
6 cloves garlic minced
1 Tbs. celery seed
1 tsp. salt
¼ tsp. pepper
1 tsp. rosemary
2-3 wild ducks skinned and split in halves

The night before, combine the first 8 ingredients in a small saucepan. Simmer for 10 minutes or so over medium-low heat. The next day, place the halved ducks into two large 1-gallon Ziploc® bags. Divide the marinade between the two and let sit for at least 12 hours. Grill over hot coals, turning occasionally until done.

Roasted Orange Duck with Wild Rice Stuffing

1 large whole duck (or small goose) plucked with skin attached
Orange peels from about 6 oranges

Stuffing

1 cup uncooked natural wild or brown rice
2½ cups chicken stock
1 small yellow onion
4 slices bacon
1 Tbs. butter
3 bay leaves
1 tsp. oregano
1½ cups chopped celery
¼ cup chopped mushrooms

Cook rice according to directions using chicken stock. Cook bacon in a skillet then remove when crisp and let drain on paper towel. Remove all but one tablespoon of grease from the skillet then add 1 tablespoon of butter along with onions, celery, mushrooms and bay leaves. Cook until onions become soft. Remove bay leaves and add 1½ cups of the cooked rice along with oregano then season with salt and pepper.

Take some of the orange peels and cut them into about 12 strips (about a ¼" wide and 1" long). With a small bladed sharp knife, cut small holes in the duck breast (about 1½ inches square). Using the point of the knife, push the orange peel down into the holes. Stuff the duck with the stuffing, cover the bottom of a roasting pan with some of the orange peels, and place the duck on top of the peels. Now cover the rest of the duck with orange peels, making sure to cover the sides of the duck until it is completely covered. Roast at 350 degrees for about 60 minutes (about 20 minutes per pound for medium). Remove duck when cooked as desired, discard orange peels, and serve.

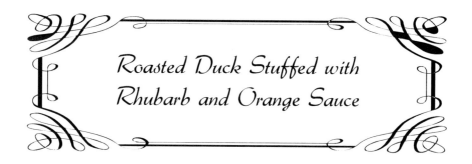

Roasted Duck Stuffed with Rhubarb and Orange Sauce

1 whole duck (or small goose) skinned
2 lb. rhubarb (6 cups chopped)
1½ cups honey
3 Tbs. cinnamon

Orange sauce

2 Tbs. butter
2 Tbs. flour
1 cup orange juice
1 Tbs. honey
1 tsp. sea salt

Cut and dice rhubarb then mix with cinnamon and honey and stuff into the duck. In a large Dutch oven or other lidded pot, add one cup of water and place stuffed duck into the pot. Cover the duck with the remaining mixed rhubarb, making sure the top of the duck is covered with at least 2 inches of stuffing. Cover with a lid and place into a pre-heated 350-degree oven. Cook for 2-3 hours, checking to make sure it does not burn or get dry (add more water if needed). The duck should be well done and almost falling off the bone when done.

Put butter into a pan and brown then add the flour and make a rue (it should be golden brown). Stir in orange juice and stir until it is smooth. Add a tablespoon of honey and 1 teaspoon of sea salt and again stir until smooth and thickened. Remove duck from the oven and cut into serving pieces. Drizzle the sauce over the duck and serve with the stuffing.

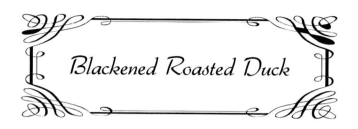

Blackened Roasted Duck

2 ducks skin attached and cut into pieces (breasts, thighs,
    legs, and wings)
Marinade
2 cups 100% cane syrup
½ cup dark molasses
¼ cup soy sauce
¼ cup balsamic vinegar
½ cup water
2 tablespoons sesame oil
¼ cup minced green onions
2 Tbs. peeled and chopped fresh ginger
1 tsp. sea salt
½ tsp. cayenne pepper
¼ tsp. coarse ground black pepper

Mix all ingredients together then add the duck and seal in a large Ziploc®
bag. Refrigerate overnight, turning the bag over several times. The next
day, drain the duck pieces in a colander (reserving the marinade). Pour
the marinade into a saucepan and simmer over medium-low heat until
it is thick and dark (about 30-40 minutes) and set it aside. Pre-heat the
oven to 350 degrees.

Heat a large skillet over high heat with no oil. Add the duck pieces, skin
side down. Cook in batches and sear until the skin is crisp, brown, and
caramelized (no more than 3-4 minutes) then turn them over and sear

for about 3 more minutes. Transfer to a wire rack set on a baking pan lined with parchment paper. When all the pieces are cooked, place the backing pan in the oven and bake for 35 minutes. Remove from the oven and smear all the pieces with the marinade then bake for another 20-25 minutes (or until the juices run clear).

Duck Shack Hoagies

After a very cold, wet morning of shooting ducks on the lower Columbia River in December, there is nothing better than returning to a nice warm and dry duck shack and making a duck hoagie.

1 duck breast per hoagie (deboned, skinned, and rinsed)
1 hoagie roll per person
1 Tbs. olive oil
Butter
2 roasted marinated red peppers
Sweet onion
Cream cheese
Tabasco sauce

Heat oil in a hot cast iron pan and fry the duck breast (about 2 minutes per side). Splash with Tabasco sauce and add sliced onion and peppers. Cook for about 5 minutes and remove from the pan. Cut open the hoagie rolls, butter the open face and place face side down into the pan until the butter just starts to melt and the rolls get slightly toasted. Pull the rolls out and slice the cream cheese, laying the slices on the bottom of the roll. Don't try to spread the cheese—just leave it in slabs. Slice the duck breast, laying the duck on top of the cream cheese, and top with the onions and peppers. Flip the top on and serve.

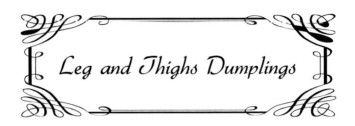

Leg and Thighs Dumplings

2 lbs. of legs and thighs from upland game birds (whole birds work well for this dish also as will a whole chicken)
2 cloves garlic
1 large onion cut in two halves
2 carrots
2 stalks of celery
6 cups water
Bisquick

Place legs and thighs in a stockpot along with garlic and half of the onion. Cover with water (at least 6 cups worth), bring to a boil, then reduce heat and simmer for about 2 hours. Remove legs and thighs from stock and allow to cool. Chop carrots, celery, and the second half of the onion and add to the stockpot. Salt and pepper to taste, pull meat from bones, and add back into the stock. Following the directions for the Bisquick, make dough for dumplings and add to the stock. Cover and cook for about 10-15 minutes or until the dumplings are set.

Sauce

1 Tbs. Worcestershire sauce
1 Tbs. Heinz 57 sauce
1 Tbs. mushroom catsup
1 Tbs. lemon juice
3 green onions or scallions chopped
2 cloves
½ tsp. mace
Pinch cayenne pepper
1½ cups chicken stock
6-8 oz. port wine

Ducks

2 fat mallards or pintails plucked
1 onion halved
12 juniper berries, crushed
¼ cup melted butter
1 tsp. grated orange rind
¼ cup red wine

Put all the sauce ingredients (except the wine) in a saucepan, bring to a boil, and simmer for 10 minutes. Add the wine and bubble again. Set aside. Melt 3 tablespoons butter and stir in 2 tablespoons flour. Cook 1-2 minutes then stir in the liquid off heat. Return to heat and stir. Bring to a boil then simmer for 5 minutes.

Stuff the cavities of each duck with ½ onion and 6 crushed juniper berries. Put ducks on a spit or rotisserie and broil for 20-30 minutes, basting often with a mixture of the melted butter, grated orange and red wine. Allow to rest, cut into serving pieces, and serve with the sauce.

Crispy Duck Chinese Style

1 4-5 lb. duck skin attached
1 whole star anise (8 cloves)
1½ Tbs. honey
1 tsp. lemon juice
2 slices ginger root
½ cup soy sauce
¼ cup ginger wine
6 cups oil

Wash and dry the duck inside and out with paper towels. In a small pan combine all the seasonings and bring to a boil for five minutes. Remove from heat and let cool for 10-15 minutes. Place the duck in a large Ziploc® bag and pour in the sauce. Marinate the duck in the sauce overnight, turning frequently.

Preheat oven to 375 degrees. Place the duck in a roasting pan and cover with foil. Bake for 1½ to 2 hours. Keep the foil on the duck only for the first hour of cooking. Remove the duck from the oven and allow to cool for 10 minutes. Reserve the sauce from the roasting pan for later use.

Rub the duck with soy sauce and honey. Split the duck in half and dust with cornstarch. Drop into hot oil until crisp. Drain and chop into small pieces for serving.

Brown sauce

Remove 3 tablespoons of soy sauce from the marinated duck mixture and add ½ teaspoon cornstarch. In a heated pan with the sauce from the baked duck, add the soy sauce and cornstarch mixture. Stir and cook until the sauce becomes clear and thickens. Pour over chopped duck and serve.

Seafood

Baked Salmon

1 whole salmon fillet
⅓ cup mayonnaise
1 sliced onion
Dill
Sea salt and pepper

Line a baking dish with foil and lay salmon fillet skin side down. Cover the fillet with mayonnaise and sprinkle with Dill. Layer sliced onion over the top of the fillet and bake in the oven at 400 degrees for approximately 25 minutes. Baking time will vary depending on the thickness of the salmon fillet.

BBQ Spring Chinook

1 whole salmon fillet
Butter
Fresh lemon
Sea salt and Pepper

Make a boat out of foil big enough for the salmon to lie in and place salmon skin side down. Squeeze fresh lemon onto the salmon fillet and season lightly with sea salt and pepper. Place onto hot coals or a preheated BBQ. Cover with lid and cook for 20-25 minutes. Cooking time will vary depending on the thickness of the salmon fillet.

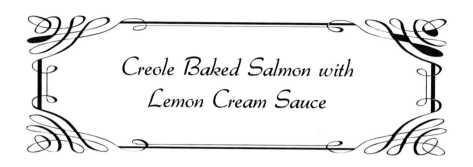

Creole Baked Salmon with Lemon Cream Sauce

1 whole fillet of salmon (bones removed, skin intact)
½ stick of butter sliced
1 lemon
Olive oil
Creole seasoning (I use Tony Chachere's Original Creole Seasoning)

Lemon Cream Sauce:

1 Tbs. butter
1 Tbs. flour
½ cup chicken broth
¼ cup heavy whipping cream
Zest of one lemon
Juice of one lemon
½ tsp. sea salt
½ tsp. sugar
⅛ tsp. white pepper
½ tsp. fresh chopped Tarragon

Preheat oven to 375 degrees. Line a baking pan with foil, apply a light amount of olive oil onto the foil and lay the salmon skin side down. Season with the Creole seasoning and place the sliced butter down the center of the fillet. Slice the lemon and lay lemon slices on top of the butter. Place in the oven and cook for 25 minutes. Remove to a platter.

With a spatula, gently slide the salmon onto a platter. The skin should stay on the foil.

In a small saucepan melt the butter over medium-high heat. Add the flour, whisking to combine, and cook for 2 minutes or until the flour is golden brown. Reduce the heat to medium, stir in the broth and cream, and simmer until thickened, whisking frequently (about 3 minutes). Add the lemon zest, lemon juice, salt, pepper, sugar, and Tarragon, whisking to combine. Cook for about 2 more minutes, whisking constantly. Pour into a serving dish and serve with the salmon.

Pan Seared Sturgeon

1 lb. sturgeon cut into about 1" cubes
2 fresh Romano tomatoes diced
1 clove garlic chopped
2 small leeks (or 1 large leek) sliced
2 Tbs. olive oil

In a cast iron skillet, heat olive oil. Add garlic and leeks then add the sturgeon. Cook for about 6-10 minutes then add the tomatoes. Season with sea salt and pepper and serve.

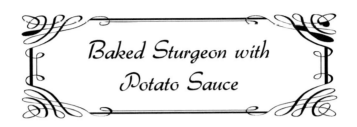

Baked Sturgeon with Potato Sauce

5-6 lb. sturgeon roast, 4-5" thick (skin and fat removed)
Sea salt and pepper
Cayenne pepper

Potato Sauce

1 cup milk
1½ cups cooked mashed potatoes
½ tsp. salt
¼ tsp. ground pepper
1 tsp. vinegar
½ tsp. cayenne pepper

Wipe the roast well and dust with salt, pepper, and cayenne pepper. Place sturgeon on a rack in a closed pan and bake at 350 degrees for 45 minutes. While baking, prepare the potato sauce.

Heat the milk and beat into mashed potatoes, butter, cayenne pepper, and salt and pepper. The sauce should almost be the consistency of mayonnaise; if it is too thick, add a little more milk. Beat the vinegar into the sauce just before serving. Pour sauce over the baked sturgeon and serve.

Grilled Shrimp

2 lb. large shrimp
2 tbs. olive oil
3 cloves garlic minced
¾ tsp. sea salt
¾ stick butter
2 tsp. chili powder
2 tsp. black pepper
4 tsp. Worcestershire sauce
1 Tbs. fresh lemon juice

Rinse shrimp. Cut down the back of the tail with scissors and devein but leave the shells on. Place shrimp in a large bowl and add olive oil, garlic, and ½ teaspoon sea salt. Toss then cover and let sit for 15 minutes. In a small pan add butter, chili powder, pepper, Worcestershire sauce and remaining ¼ teaspoon sea salt. Cook over medium heat until butter is melted. Remove from heat and stir in lemon juice.

Thread 4-5 shrimp onto a bamboo skewer and grill, turning over once until just cooked through (about 3-4 minutes). Remove shrimp from skewers onto a serving dish, cover with the melted butter mixture, toss, and serve.

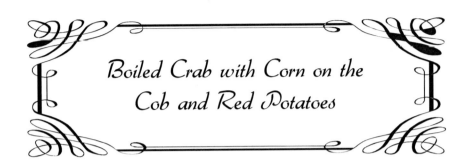

Boiled Crab with Corn on the Cob and Red Potatoes

12 live Dungeness crab
12 fresh corn on the cob
12 red potatoes
Old Bay seasoning (1 heaping tablespoon per gallon)
Sea salt or fresh salt water from the beach
    (1 cup per gallon of fresh water)
Pot large enough to boil the crab (I use an old beer keg)

Bring salt water to a boil. Add the Old Bay seasoning and crab and bring back to a boil. Cook for 15 minutes after the water returns to a boil. After 15 minutes remove the crab and plunge them into cold water. Add the whole potatoes to the crab pot and allow to boil for about 15 minutes. In the meantime, back the crabs. (Clean them by removing the backs, gills, etc.) When all the crabs are cleaned place them back into the crab pot with the corn, turn the heat off, and allow to sit for 5-10 minutes.

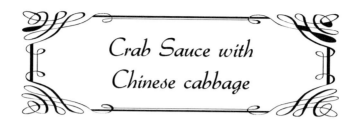

Crab Sauce with Chinese cabbage

2 lb. Chinese cabbage
2-3 slices of fresh ginger root
2 garlic cloves
3 Tbs. cooking oil
1½ tsp. salt
1 tsp. sugar
1 tsp. coarse black pepper

Seasoning for Crab Sauce

1 lb. crabmeat
4 Tbs. sesame oil
3 Tbs. flour
3 Tbsp. Ginger wine or regular dry wine
2 cups chicken stock
3 Tbs. milk
2 chopped green onion

Wash and cut cabbage into strips 2" long by 1" wide. Heat 3 tablespoons oil in a wok. When oil is hot add ginger and garlic cloves and cook until garlic is nice and brown, but not burned. Remove garlic and ginger from pan. Turn heat to high and add cabbage, salt, pepper, and sugar. Cook until cabbage starts to turn soft. Remove from wok, place in a strainer, and allow to sit. Clean out the wok and add the 4 tablespoons sesame oil. When oil is hot, add flour and stir. Cook until flour is nice and brown then add ginger wine, chicken stock, and milk. Allow to thicken but do not boil. When the sauce starts to thicken, add crab and cabbage. Softly stir to mix, allow to thicken and serve.

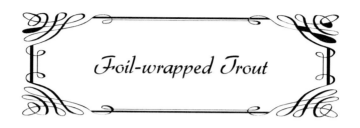

Foil-wrapped Trout

When I was a kid, my Mom and Dad would take off for some alone time occasionally, leaving my sisters and I with Grandma and Grandpa. On one of those occasions, Grandpa decided to take me fishing on the Yamhill River. The first thing Grandpa did was build a small fire on the bank of the river. After we had caught a couple of fish, Grandpa gathered some Maple leaves and after gutting the trout, he wrapped them in the maple leafs and then clay from the bank of the river. He placed the wrapped fish in the coals and then built the fire up on top of them. We continued to fish for about another hour until the mud had hardened and then it was time to break the mold and eat the fish. Grandpa said this is how the Indians had cooked their fish and he had learned it as a kid. Being the smart 8-year-old I was at the time, I mentioned to Grandpa that there was a thing called tinfoil. Grandpa actually smirked before he smacked me. I love fishing small streams and I always carry foil, butter and lemon pepper seasonings in my fishing gear for this streamside lunch.

Trout
Foil
Butter
Lemon pepper

Gut the trout and season with lemon pepper. Place slices of butter inside the trout and wrap with foil. Place wrapped fish in the coals of a fire and turn after 3-4 minutes (depending the size of the fish). Cook for another 3-4 minutes and remove from coals. Carefully unwrap and eat.

Snake River Catfish

½ cup cornmeal
½ cup flour, sifted
1 tsp. salt
¼ tsp. pepper
⅛ tsp. ginger
2 eggs
Catfish fillets
Vegetable oil (for frying)

In a bowl, mix cornmeal, flour, salt, pepper, and ginger. In a separate bowl, beat the eggs. Dip the catfish fillets into the eggs then coat both sides with the cornmeal mixture. In a heavy cast iron skillet, add oil and heat to around 360 degrees. Fry the coated catfish until coating turns nice and brown—do not overcook.

Pasta and Rice Dishes

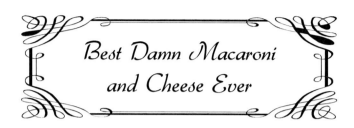

Best Damn Macaroni and Cheese Ever

2 cups uncooked macaroni noodles
1 can cream of chicken soup
½ cup milk
¼ cup Marsala wine
¼ cup grated Parmigianino cheese
½ cup grated cheddar cheese
½ cup grated Swiss cheese

Boil noodles until cooked, al dente. Drain and place into a greased casserole dish. Add cream of chicken soup, milk, and Marsala wine to a bowl. Grate all the cheese and mix in as well. Add the noodles, mix, and place into the oven at 400 degrees for 25-35 minutes or until top is browned.

Garlic Butter and Sweet Basil Pasta

For this recipe, I like a pasta with some room in it, like a Penne, Rotini, or Fusilli, is ideal. This way, the garlic and cheese have a place to hang out until they meet your taste buds.

1 box pasta
4 cloves garlic sliced thin
1 sweet yellow onion
1 bunch fresh basil leaves rough cut (about 1 heaping cup)
1 tsp. fresh oregano leaves only
1 tsp. fresh rosemary stemmed
1 stick of butter
1 Tbs. sea salt
6 Tbs. olive oil
1 cup fresh grated Asiago cheese
4 quarts water

In a large pot add water, sea salt, and 1 tablespoon of olive oil. Bring to a boil and add pasta. Cook until al dente. While the pasta is cooking, place remaining olive oil and butter in a large frying pan. Bring to medium heat, add garlic and onion, and cook until onions are soft and starting to turn. When pasta is cooked, drain and add to the frying pan, reduce heat, then add basil, rosemary and oregano. Stir to coat and slowly add the grated Asiago cheese until all of the cheese is added. Taste and adjust seasonings with sea salt and more Asiago cheese.

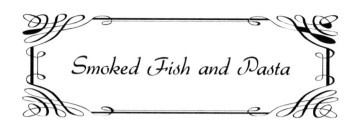

Smoked Fish and Pasta

1 can or 1 lb. of smoked fish (smoked trout, sturgeon or
   salmon work well)
1 package pasta
½ stick butter
1 Tbs. olive oil
4 cloves garlic
1 small sweet yellow onion
1 small lemon
½ teaspoon sugar
3 cups uncooked spinach leaves
Asiago cheese

Boil water for pasta and cook until done. While the pasta is cooking, add butter and olive oil to a saucepan and cook on low heat. Cut garlic and onion and add to butter. Let simmer on low heat until the garlic and onion are soft. Add juice, zest of lemon, and sugar and continue to simmer until the pasta is cooked. Drain pasta and place in a serving bowl. Add spinach to butter and stir until it just starts to wilt, then add smoked fish and pour over pasta with grated cheese. Gently mix so as not to break up the fish and serve.

Razor Clams Alfredo

1 lb. frozen razor clams, juice included—¼ cup will be needed for the recipe; use clam juice from a bottle if needed
1 lb. linguine spaghetti
1 Tbs. chopped fresh oregano
1 Tbs. chopped fresh rosemary
2 Tbs. chopped fresh basil
3 cloves minced garlic
1 large leek, sliced thin (white and about half of the green)
¼ cup Marsala wine
3 Tbs. flour
1 cup cold water
2 cups milk or cream
1 Tbs. butter
2 Tbs. olive oil
Sea salt and pepper to taste

In a large stockpot, add enough water to cook the linguine, salt, and 1 tablespoon olive oil. Bring to a boil and cook the linguine until al dente (about 12-15 minutes).

While the linguine is cooking, add butter and remaining 1 tablespoon olive oil to a medium-large heated sauté pan. Add minced garlic, oregano, rosemary, basil, and leek. Cook for about 2 minutes. Chop razor clams and add to pan with the clam juice and the Marsala wine. Mix the flour into cold water until the flour is completely dissolved; it should look like watered down milk. Increase the heat to medium-high and slowly add the flour mixture to the pan, stirring until the juices become thickened. Reduce heat and slowly add the milk into the pan while stirring. Allow to simmer; a gentle bubble is OK. When Linguine is al dente, drain and add to the clams and toss and serve.

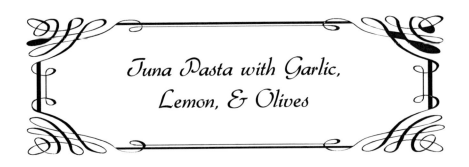

Tuna Pasta with Garlic, Lemon, & Olives

3 cups dried conchiglie or gnocchi pasta
4 Tbs. olive oil
4 Tbs. butter
3-4 garlic cloves sliced thin
7 oz. canned tuna
2 Tbs. lemon juice
10-12 black olives pitted and sliced
2 Tbs. flat-leaf parsley chopped fresh
Fresh Romano cheese shavings (to garnish)

Cook the pasta in salted water until al dente. Drain and return to the pan.

Heat olive oil and half the butter in a skillet over low-medium heat. Add the garlic and cook until the garlic just begins to turn color. Reduce heat and add tuna, lemon juice, and olives. Stir gently until all is heated through. Add the cooked pasta to the tuna mixture Add the parsley and remaining butter then toss and top with Romano cheese shavings.

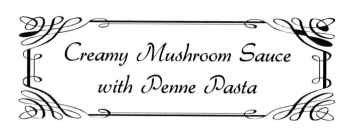

Creamy Mushroom Sauce with Penne Pasta

4 Tbs. butter
1 Tbs. olive oil
1 leek sliced
1 lb. mushrooms sliced
Sea salt and pepper
1 tsp. flour
½ cup cream
2 Tbs. Marsala wine or Port
4 oz. sun-dried tomatoes in oil, drained and chopped
Pinch of freshly grated nutmeg
12 oz. dried Penne pasta
2 Tbs. flat leaf parsley chopped

Melt the butter with the olive oil in a large heavy-bottom skillet. Add the leeks and cook over low heat, stirring occasionally until softened. Add the mushrooms and cook over low heat for about 3-4 minutes. Season with salt and pepper, sprinkle in the flour, and cook for about 1 minute. Remove skillet from the heat and gradually stir in cream and wine. Return to the heat and add sun-dried tomatoes and grated nutmeg and cook over low heat, stirring occasionally, for about 10 minutes.

Meanwhile, cook the penne pasta in salted water until al dente Drain the pasta well and add to the mushroom sauce. Cook for about 3-5 minutes, sprinkle with chopped parsley, and serve out of the pan.

Dirty Rice

2 cups uncooked rice
1 large sweet yellow onion
2 cloves minced garlic
1 lb. venison burger or any meat
4-5 chicken livers or Rabbit livers *Optional
4 green onions cut up fine
½ teaspoon red pepper
Sea salt to taste
4 strips bacon fried crisp and broken into small pieces (reserve drippings)
⅓ cup chopped fresh cilantro or parsley
6 cups water

Cook the rice until just barely done (the rice should be soft but moist). Cook the bacon until crisp and remove to a paper towel. Chop the onion fine and add to the bacon drippings along with garlic. Add the burger and livers and cook until it is just barely done. Add cilantro, salt and red pepper, and rice. Crumble the bacon into the rice and add the chopped green onion. Cook until the moisture is absorbed. Stir slowly and serve.

Wild Rice

1 cup wild rice uncooked
1 bay leaf
1 tsp. oregano
2 celery stalks chopped
½ lb. mushrooms chopped
1 leek chopped
2 Tbs. butter
2½ cups beef broth

Add butter, leek, mushrooms, and celery to a large pot and simmer for about 5 minutes. Add wild rice, bay leaf, and beef broth and bring to a boil. Cover and reduce heat. Simmer for about 40 minutes (check toward the end of the time so the rice does not burn). Cook until the liquid is absorbed or cooked off. Season and serve.

Spanish Rice

2 cups uncooked Jasmine rice
1 medium sweet yellow onion chopped fine
3 cloves garlic chopped fine
3 Tbs. olive oil
1 can diced tomatoes juice and all
¼ cup sliced black olives
2 cups chicken broth

In a large pan heat olive oil and add onion and garlic. Cook until onions are clear and the garlic starts to turn color. Add rice and cook until rice starts to turn color—it will start to look golden and the garlic will be brown. Add chicken broth, tomatoes, and olives. Stir and bring to a gentle boil. Cover and reduce heat to low—**do not** stir the rice again. Let simmer for about 30-35 minutes, check, and when all of the liquid is absorbed remove and serve.

Aunt Alice's Rice

1 stick of butter
¼ cup chopped onion
1 can beef consume'
½ cup water
1 cup rice

Melt butter in skillet and sauté onion until clear. Add the rice and cook until it just starts to turn. Add beef broth and water then cover. Bake at 350 degrees for 1 hour.

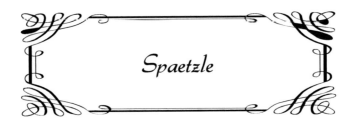

Spaetzle

2¼ cups flour
½ tsp. salt
¼ tsp. baking powder
¼ tsp. nutmeg
2 eggs
1 cup milk
Salted water

Sift flour, salt, baking powder, and nutmeg. Beat eggs into milk and add to the flour mixture. Mix well. Crank the batter through the holes in a spaetzle machine or push it through a colander (or just cut it up into very fine little noodles).

In a large stockpot, bring water to a boil. Cook the spaetzle for about 1-1½ minutes (until the little noodles rise to the surface or until tender). Drain, rinse with hot water, and serve.

"That Was Good!
What is it?!"

My Dad once told me "Hunger is the greatest spice known to man. With it you can eat anything."

Our primitive forefathers gathered and ate a lot of things that often make their modern day children say "Yuck." So, if you are one of those people who say they don't like something just because of what it is then this chapter is not for you. Over the years I have eaten a lot of things my buddies called bait: Eels' smelt, herring, bugs, grubs and a lot wild plants some people would call weeds. Here are some of my favorite unusual recipes and I think you will find that you do not have to be starving to enjoy them.

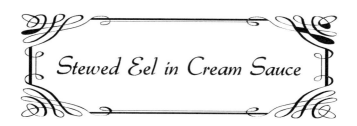

Stewed Eel in Cream Sauce

¼ lb. salt pork cut into ½" cubes
3 lbs. eel cut into 3" pieces
1 Tbs. chopped shallots
1 carrot sliced
1 rib celery diced
1½ cup's dry white wine
¼ cup applejack or brandy
1 tsp. salt
6 peppercorns
1 bay leaf
¼ tsp. powdered thyme
¼ tsp. tarragon
¼ tsp. marjoram
½ tsp. sage
3 Tbs. butter
1½ Tbs. flour
2 egg yolks beaten
½ cup heavy cream
Juice of ½ lemon

Fry out the fat of the salt pork cubes in a saucepan. Remove and reserve the cracklings and all but 2-3 tablespoons of the fat. Add eel pieces and brown on all sides, then add the shallots, carrot, and celery, and cook for 3-4 minutes more over low to medium heat.

Add wine, applejack or brandy, salt, peppercorns, and the five herbs. Simmer until eel pieces are just done (about 20 minutes). Remove eel pieces to a hot serving dish and strain the stock in which the eels simmered. Return to the heat and boil to reduce to 1 cup. Melt the butter in a separate saucepan or use all or part of the remaining salt pork fat to make 2 tablespoons. Stir in the flour and cook while stirring (a minute or two). Off heat, add the eel stock then cook over low heat, stirring, until sauce begins to thicken. In a bowl, mix the beaten egg yolk with the cream and spoon in several tablespoons of the hot sauce. Slowly stir the egg mixture back into the sauce, add lemon juice, and cook over very low heat until the finished sauce is thick and smooth. Do not allow it to boil. Pour the sauce over the eel and sprinkle cracklings on as a garnish.

Baked Stuffed Shad

4 lb. shad, dressed (gutted and scales removed)
1 tsp. lemon juice
Salt and pepper
Bread stuffing with sage and rosemary
2 Tbs. melted butter
1 leek, white and first part of the green finely chopped
4 strips of bacon

Rub inside and out of shad with lemon juice. Salt and pepper the fish then stuff it and skewer the cavity. Coat fish with melted butter and lay on a sheet of foil large enough to enfold the fish. Wrap the shad with bacon strips then sprinkle with the chopped leeks and enfold the shad securely with the foil. Place the foiled shad in a shallow baking dish and bake at 225 degrees for 5-6 hours. The shad will come out moist, succulent, and boneless.

Coot Stew

1-2 coot, skin removed and cut into serving sized pieces
2 cups buttermilk
½ lb. bacon
2 cloves garlic smashed
1 medium onion chopped
2 ribs celery diced
½ tsp. dried basil
½ cup red wine
½ cup water

Place the coot into a crockery container large enough to hold all of it. Cover with buttermilk and marinate for 48 hours or more in a cool place. Remove the coot and wipe off excess buttermilk. Reserve the buttermilk for thickening gravy.

Over medium heat, fry bacon in a large skillet and remove when crisp. Brown the garlic in the hot bacon fat; remove before it browns. Add the onion, celery, and basil and cook until onions are soft. Add the coot and cook quickly to seal in the juices, turning once. Add water and red wine. Cook for 15-20 minutes at medium heat. Thicken liquid in the skillet with the reserved buttermilk. Serve with crusty bread.

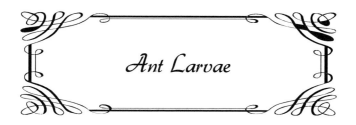

Ant Larvae

Ants are really high in protein but they are kind of bitter; the larvae, on the other hand, are really good. To gather larvae, find a big ground ant's nest, black or red. Lay a tarp on the ground by the nest and lay about six sticks (about 8" to 1' in length) in lines so you are forming traffic lanes. Take the backside of the tarp that is away from the nest and fold it over so it covers the backside of the sticks. Then kick or shovel the ant nest onto the tarp. The worker ants will start grabbing the larvae to get it out of the sun and away from danger, the ants see the traffic lanes created by the sticks and move the larvae under the folded tarp for protection. Give this about an hour then shovel or kick more of the anthill onto the tarp. In an hour or two (which is plenty of time to build a shelter or have several beers while watching the ants work) you will have a sufficient amount of ant larvae. Scoop up the larvae and pour into a bucket of clean water, what sticks and ants are still with the larvae will float to the top and you can clean them off, leaving you with just larvae.

Larvae Crispy

½-1 lb. ant larvae
Sugar
Oil (for frying)

Form the larvae into small hamburger patties. Add a little oil to a heated skillet and fry the patties to a golden brown. Remove and sprinkle with sugar. This is one of the most savory foods; it is very much like rice-crispy balls. You might think it is a lot of work that is not worth the end result, at least until you taste them.

Grilled Grasshoppers

It is best to gather the grasshoppers for this recipe in the early morning—that is the fun part.

2-3 dozen grasshoppers
3 Tbs. Soy sauce
Bamboo kabob sticks (long thin ones)

Hold grasshopper by the back, grasp the head, and pull—this will remove the head and the guts. Slide the grasshopper onto kabob stick; and yes, they will keep hopping. Stick four to six grasshoppers on each of the kabob sticks (depending on the size of the grasshoppers).

Lay the grasshopper kabobs in a large, shallow pan mix soy sauce and sugar until sugar dissolves and baste the grasshopper kabobs with the sauce. Allow to sit for 10-15 minutes then cook over high heat until crisp (about 2-3 minutes).

Yellow Jacket Soup

Yellow jacket grubs make a very nice broth and have excellent flavor.
Find a ground-dwelling yellow jacket nest, (best to do this in the early
morning or in the late afternoon). Gather the whole comb.

Place the comb over a small fire with the right side up to loosen the
grubs that are not covered. Remove all the uncovered grubs. Now place
the comb over the fire upside down until the paper like covering parches.
Remove the comb from the heat, pick out the yellow jacket grubs, and
place them in the oven to brown. Make the soup by boiling the browned
yellow jacket grubs in a pot of water with salt and little bacon grease.
Strain and serve the clear broth.

Deep-Fat-Fried Rattlesnake

When it comes to cooking with snakes, they should be at least 3 feet long. The little ones just don't have that much meat on them.

1 rattlesnake cut into 3" pieces
2 Tbs. lemon juice
¼ cup oil
1 tsp. salt

Fritter Batter

1 egg
½ cup plus 1-2 Tbs. flour
½ cup milk

Marinate snake meat in the refrigerator overnight in lemon juice. Baste meat occasionally. Wipe meat dry after marinating and dip the pieces in fritter batter (see below) Deep-fat-fry in a heavy skillet.

Fritter batter: beat together egg and milk then stir in flour. Let batter rest about 20-30 minutes. Batter should be quite runny when used, similar to fresh cream. Only a thin batter will fry crisp. Use in the above rattlesnake recipe.

Eden Bench
BBQ Rattlesnake

One year while hunting in Eastern Oregon out of Troy, I was riding in the back of the pickup truck on the tail gate drinking a beer with my feet hanging off the gate, when all of the sudden I get smacked in the back of my boot right in the heel. It felt like I had been hit with a baseball bat. I look back in the road and there is a large Rattlesnake. Gary had driven over it with the truck and it had struck me in the boot. Lucky for me, it did not bite through. Anyway, we killed the snake and after gutting and skinning him, the guys wanted to eat him. I suggested cutting up the snake but they wanted to cook him whole, (Who am I to argue?) Later that night, with the grill heated up, Kip tossed the snake on it. The snake rose up and started striking just like it was alive. I looked at it and said, "Dig in boys."

1 rattlesnake cut into 3" inch pieces
Yoshida's Original Marinade

Soak the meat in Yoshida's Original Marinade for at least an hour in a large bowl. Cook over hot grill. Note that snake cooks very quickly.

Whistle Pig Pie

1-2 young groundhogs, skinned and cleaned
1 cup yellow onion chopped
¼ cup green pepper
½ tablespoon minced parsley
1 Tbs. salt
½ tsp. pepper
4½ Tbs. flour
3 cups broth

Topping

1 cup flour
2 tsp. baking powder
¼ tsp. salt
2 Tbs. lard
¼ cup milk

Cut groundhogs into 2 or 3 pieces. Parboil for 1 hour. Remove meat from the bones, keeping them in large pieces. Add onion, green pepper, parsley, salt, pepper, and flour to the broth and stir until it thickens. If the broth does not measure 3 cups, add water. Add the meat to the broth mixture and stir thoroughly. Pour into a baking dish.

Sift the flour, baking powder, and salt together. Cut in the fat and add the liquid. Stir until the dry ingredients are moist. Roll only enough to make it fit the baking dish. Place dough on top of the meat and put the baking dish in a hot oven (400 degrees) and bake 30-40 minutes or until dough is browned.

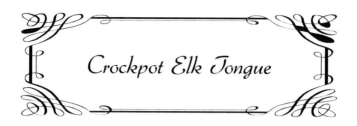

Crockpot Elk Tongue

1 elk tongue
1½ cups water
2 lemons juiced and zest
3 Tbs. coarse black pepper
1 bay leaf
2 Tbs. sea salt

Put water and tongue into a crock-pot. Add pepper, lemon juice, bay leaf, and salt. Put on low heat for 8-9 hours, peel tongue, slice, and serve. Can be served hot or cold.

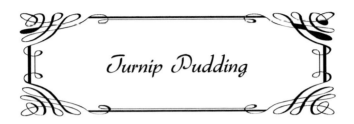

Turnip Pudding

4 large yellow turnips (rutabagas)
2 Tbs. vinegar
½ cup milk
1 egg beaten
1 Tbs. molasses
½ cup melted butter
2 Tbs. brown sugar
½ tsp. salt
½ tsp. allspice

Peel and cube the turnips and boil in salted water until tender. Drain well. Heat vinegar to boiling point then add the turnips and mash. While mashing, add all the remaining ingredients. Pour the mixture into a greased pie tin and place in a 325-degree oven for 30-35 minutes.

Rose Hip Ketchup

4 qt. rose hips red and ripe
1 clove garlic
2 med. Onions
1 cup water * or enough to cover
Boil these ingredients until soft. Strain and add ¾-cup brown sugar.

Wrap in a cheesecloth ½ Tbsp. each whole allspice, mace, whole cloves, and a 2-inch stick of cinnamon. Boil these ingredients quickly. Add 1-cup vinegar, cayenne pepper and salt to taste. Boil ketchup 10 minutes and pour into sterilized jars.

Rubies Red Cinnamon Water Melon Rinds

My mom used to make these watermelon rinds and boy are they good. They go well with wild game dishes as a side dish or garnish.

15 cups cubed Watermelon Rinds
3 cups Distilled White vinegar
1 Gallon of water
¼ cup slaked lime or calcium Hydroxide
¼ tsp. cinnamon oil
½ tsp. clove oil
7 cups white sugar
1 tsp. red food coloring
¾ cup Red hot cinnamon candies

Cut open watermelons remove red flesh and enjoy. With the rinds cut all of the green skin off and make sure all of the red flesh is removed. You will want about fifteen cups of white rind cut into about 1 inch cubes. In a large crock or pot add the gallon of water and the slaked lime and the cube watermelon; make sure there is enough water to cover and let set overnight. The next day remove the watermelon rinds and rinse off all the lime, use a metal strainer and allow to set under running water until thoroughly rinsed. When rinsed, place watermelon rinds into a large pot, cover with water and bring to a gentle boil.

Cook for about thirty minutes. Drain off water. In a large mixing bowl add the distilled vinegar, white sugar, cinnamon oil, clove oil, red food coloring, and Red Hot cinnamon candies.

Using a metal whisk rapidly stir these ingredients until the candies and sugars are dissolved. Pour over the watermelon rinds and bring to a gentle boil, reduce heat and allow to cook for about 45 minutes.

Keep an eye on it and add more water if it looks like it needs it, stir once in a while to keep it from burning. When the watermelon rinds look transparent they are done.

Place into hot sterilized jars, cover them with the hot syrup seal and process in boiling hot water bath for ten minutes.

Bread, Bannock, Biscuits, and Dough

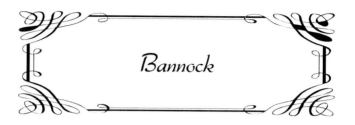

Bannock

If someone doesn't know how to make bannock then they are not a true woodsman. Bannock is nothing more than pan bread. It is easy to make and goes with anything because you can add anything to it—from dried fruit to chopped onions, chilies, and cheese. Here is a basic bannock recipe.

4 cups flour
2 tsp. baking powder
½ tsp. baking soda
½ tsp. salt
4 Tbs. butter or lard
1½ cups milk

Mix the dry ingredients together in a bowl. Cut the butter or lard into the mix, using your fingers to crumble the mix until it is pebbly. Make a hole in the center and pour the liquid in all at once. Mix it then gather around the edges of the mix with a fork until it all comes together into one lump of dough. Knead it five or six times quickly and turn out onto a floured board. Shape and pat into a circle at least ½" thick. Bake in a lightly greased medium-hot skillet or on a griddle (about 10 minutes each side).

Campfire Bannock

2 cups flour
2 heaping tsp. baking powder
Pinch of salt
1 cup dried milk
4 heaping tsp. sugar

Add enough water to wet all ingredients, but not enough to make it runny. Put 4 tbs. lard or bacon grease in a hot pan and cook on a slow coal fire. When one side is done, turn over and cook the other side.

Pocket Scones

There is nothing better than being in the woods before the sun comes up, sitting on stand. The only thing that makes it even better is having a small thermos of coffee and a couple of these pocket scones.

2 cups flour
1 Tbs. baking powder
2 Tbs. sugar
½ tsp. salt
½ tsp. powdered cinnamon
¼ tsp. powdered ginger
3 Tbs. butter or lard
1 egg
½ cup milk
3 Tbs. Molasses
½ cup raisins, currants or finely chopped dried apricots or dates (whichever type of dried fruit that is preferred)

Combine and sift flour, baking powder, sugar, salt, and spices into a bowl. Blend in the butter or lard using your fingers. In another bowl, beat the egg until well beaten. Add milk and molasses then mix well. Make a hole in the center of the dry mix and pour in liquid. While mixing and gathering into a lump of dough, sprinkle in and then mix in the dried fruit. Turn out onto a lightly floured surface. Knead a few times, pat out into ½ inch thick circles, and then cut the circles into wedges. Bake on top of the stove in a lightly greased skillet or on a griddle. When cooled, the wedges or scones can be packaged separately and carried in your jacket pocket for snacking along the trail.

Sourdough Starter

Two important things to remember when cooking sourdough started:

1. *Always take out 1 cup of the mix and save it to start your next batch (called starter).*

2. *Never (and I mean never) add anything to your sourdough starter except water and flour. Sourdough smells sour, so don't panic and throw it out. If it smells too ripe, freshen it by adding 2 cups warm water and 2½ cups flour. Save 1 cup and throw out the rest.*

Starter

3 cups white flour
1 package dry yeast

Peel and boil potatoes allow to cool and remove 2½ cups lukewarm potato water use the potatoes for something else, you only need the water.

Sourdough pot *(always use a glass or crock container that has a good-fitting lid)

Mix flour, yeast, and potato water in a large bowl. Beat until all the lumps are gone. Pour into the sourdough pot and cover with lid (not tightly). Let sit at room temperature for 3-4 days—until it smells like vinegar. When not in use, keep the sourdough starter in a cool place. When ready to use, bring it out the night before. Add flour and water the next day.

Sourdough Bread

The night before baking, add to starter:
2½ cups flour
2 cups lukewarm water

Beat until smooth, cover, and sit in a warm place overnight. In the morning, take out 1 cup of sourdough for starter. Add the following to the remaining dough:

4 cups white flour unsifted
1 tsp. salt
2 Tbs. sugar
½ tsp. baking soda
3 Tbs. oil or bacon drippings

Mix thoroughly. If needed, add more flour to achieve a suitable sough for kneading. Turn dough onto a well-floured board and knead until satiny and smooth (about 10-12 minutes). Put dough into a well-greased bowl, cover with a clean hand towel, and let sit in warm place to rise for about 2½ hours (or until doubled in size). Punch down the dough and shape into 1 large round loaf or 2 small French loaves. Sprinkle a well-greased cookie sheet with cornmeal and place the loaves on the sheet. Cover with a clean hand towel and let rise until double the size (about 1 hour). Preheat oven to 400 degrees. Add 1-2 cups of water to a ovenproof container and put it in the lower part of the oven. Place bread in the oven and bake for 45-50 minutes or until golden brown. The steam from the water will give the bread a nice crust.

Sourdough Bannock

1 cup sourdough starter
2 cups water
¾ cup cornmeal
¾ cup white flour
3 Tbs. dried milk
2 eggs
4 Tbs. brown sugar
1 Tbs. molasses
4 Tbs. melted butter
½ cup dried apricots or dates, chopped
½ tsp. salt
½ tsp. baking soda

The night before: Take a cup of starter from your starter pot and put it in a bowl with 1½ cups water, cornmeal, and flour. Stir but do not beat. Let stand overnight, partly covered.

In the morning: Make a paste of the dried milk and ½ cup water and stir into the mix. Then beat the eggs and stir them in the mix along with sugar, molasses, and melted butter. Then add the apricots or dates.

Add salt and baking soda to the mixture just before ladling the batter into a well-greased hot cast-iron skillet. Bake on top of the stove over a fairly hot plate for 10 minutes, shaking it after it sets to loosen it, then flip it over and bake the other side. This can also be baked in an oven. Bake at 450 degrees for about 30 minutes.

Every year when the Clackamas county fair came around, Mom would enter her paintings and dad would enter his Bread. Now they both won a lot of ribbons, but Dad won best of show 7 years in a row.

Joe's French Bread

8-Cups warm water
4-Packs Dry yeast
1 ½ tsp. powdered ginger
8 tsp. salt
4 Tbs. sugar
8 cups flour

In a bowl add the warm water (110) degrees or less and the yeast stir until yeast is dissolved. To a large mixing bowl add the flour, salt, sugar and ginger mix well and then add the water and yeast. Mix by hand until smooth and elastic. On a floured board place dough and knead for about 10 minutes adding more flour a little at a time as necessary. Dough should be stiff. Form dough into a ball. Using olive oil grease the inside of a large bowl, rub the outside of the dough ball with the left over oil on your hands and place the dough ball into the greased bowl, cover with a loose cloth and place in a warm place allow dough to rise until double in size, about 1 ½ hours. Break the rise by punching down the dough while it is still in the bowl. Place dough onto a lightly floured surface cut into equal sections and form into desired shape of loafs.

Lightly grease a cookie sheet dust with corn meal and place a loaf on the cookie sheet. With an egg yolk wash brush the top of the loaf and then with a sharp knife make 3-4 slashes diagonally across the top of the loafs. Let rise again until double in size.

Preheat the oven to 325 degrees and bake for 25-30 minutes or until bread sounds hollow when thumped. Cool on a rack.

*For a chewy crust place a small pan of water in the oven when baking the bread.

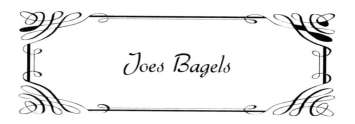

Joes Bagels

1 package dry active yeast
1 ½ cups warm water (105-110) degrees
3 Tbs. sugar
1 Tbs. salt
4 ½ cups flour
1 gallon water

Stir yeast into warm water and let set until yeast is bubbly and dissolved. In a large bowl add flour, sugar and salt mix and then add the dissolved yeast. Mix by hand and then knead dough on a floured board by hand adding flour if needed until dough is smooth and elastic. Let dough rest and rise for about twenty minutes. Punch dough down and roll onto a lightly floured surface to a rectangle 13-14 inches and about 1 inch thick. Cut into strips and roll each strip into a rope. It should be about 1 inch thick and about 6 inches in length, now take the rope and roll it around one hand with both ends connecting under your hand gently roll until the ends are fused together. Place onto a floured cookie sheet until all of the bagels are formed; cover with a loose cloth and let rise for about twenty minutes.

In a large stock pot bring a gallon of water to a boil. Reduce heat to medium and Place 3-4 bagels into the water simmer uncovered for about 3 to 7-minutes flipping the bagels about half way through. Place bagels on a drying or cooling rack, repeat until all the bagels have been boiled.

Pre-heat oven to 375 degrees place bagels on ungreased cookie sheet and bake for about 30-35 minutes or until golden brown. Cool on a wire rack.

Makes about 18 bagels

*To top bagels with poppy seeds or sesame seeds remove bagels from oven after 10 minutes of baking, beat one egg white with 1 Tbs. water and brush the tops of the bagels with the mixture and sprinkle with desired topping, place bagels back into oven and bake until golden brown. If you want to add flavors such as raisins, peppers, onions, or herbs add them to the dough while kneading. One other thing to remember about bagels, the longer you boil them the chewier they will be.

Potato Yeast Biscuits

1 qt. scalded milk
1 cup mashed potatoes
1 cake quick-rising yeast
1 tsp. soda
2 tsp. baking powder
1 cup lard (bear lard if lucky)
½ cup sugar
2 tsp. salt

Mix lard, mashed potatoes, and scalded milk. Let cool. Add sugar and yeast dissolved in warm water, then flour (enough to make batter). Let rise then add salt, soda, and baking powder. Beat batter thoroughly and add enough flour to make it the consistency of biscuit dough. Let rise and cut into biscuits. Let rise again. Bake for 10 minutes in a 400-degree preheated oven.

Buttermilk Biscuits

2¼ cups flour
⅓ tsp. baking soda
1 tsp. salt
2 tsp. baking powder
5 Tbs. lard
1 cup buttermilk

Sift and mix dry ingredients then blend with lard. Add buttermilk. To make each biscuit, pinch off a portion of dough about the size of a large egg and pat out with your hands. Bake at 475-500 degrees for about 10 minutes.

Homemade Bisquick

My good friend Carrie Bergin's grandpa created Bisquick and gave the recipe to a friend of his—that guy made a lot of dough.

8 cups sifted flour
4 Tbs. baking powder
2 cups powdered milk
1 cup lard
1½ tsp. salt
3 Tbs. white sugar

Mix all of the dry ingredients well then cut in the lard until well mixed. Place in a covered container and keep in a cool place. Make ahead of time for camping or hunting trips.

For pancakes: Add water and eggs. Mix to a pancake mixture.
For hot biscuits: Add water and mix to biscuit consistency.
For cake: Add water, eggs, and vanilla.

Pizza Dough

This dough recipe will make two 12" pizza crusts.

1 package active dry yeast
1 cup warm water mixed with 1 Tbs. sugar
3 cups all-purpose flour
1 tsp. salt
2 Tbs. olive oil
¼ cup cornmeal (for baking)

In a large mixing bowl, sprinkle yeast over water and stir until dissolved. Place in a warm location for 5 minutes to activate yeast. Add remaining ingredients, mixing in each ingredient one at a time. Place dough on a floured surface and knead until smooth and elastic. Form into a ball, brush top with a little olive oil and place in a greased bowl. Cover and let sit in a warm location for about 1½ hours or until dough has doubled. Cut dough in half and roll out to form shells. Cover with desired toppings.

Preheat oven to 500 degrees. Place pizza stone (if available) in the oven to preheat. A baking sheet can be used instead as well. Place corn meal on stone or baking sheet just before placing the pizza in the oven.

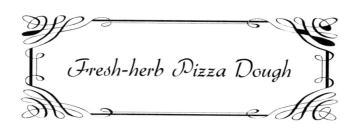

Fresh-herb Pizza Dough

This recipe will make about six 6" pizzas and really good bread sticks.

1¾ cups plus 1 Tbs. warm water
1 package active dry yeast
2½ cups white flour
¾ cup semolina flour
1 Tbs. salt
¼ cup mixed chopped fresh herbs (I use rosemary, oregano, basil, and thyme)
2 Tbs. olive oil
¼ cup cornmeal (for baking)

In a large bowl, combine water and yeast and let stand for 5 minutes to activate the yeast. Add to the yeast mixture, bread flour, semolina flour, salt, herbs, and olive oil. Mix by hand until well mixed. (A mixer with a bread hook can be used if available.) Place on a floured surface and knead until smooth and elastic. Roll into a ball and lightly cover with a little olive oil. Place in a greased bowl and cover. Let rise in a warm place for 1½ to 2 hours or until doubled in size.

Punch down dough and cut into six portions. Form into 6 balls and cover with a towel while rolling out each pizza.

On a floured surface, roll out each ball into a 6" circle. Top with desired toppings. Preheat oven to 500 degrees. Place a pizza stone on the middle rack to pre-heat. I use an old Granite tile that is 12x12". A baking sheet can be used as well.

Desserts

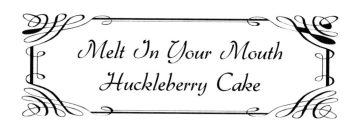

Melt In Your Mouth Huckleberry Cake

4 egg whites
½ cup sugar
1cup shortening
½ tsp. salt
2 tsp. vanilla
4 egg yolks
1½ cups sugar
3 cups flour
3 cups fresh or frozen huckleberries
2 tsp. baking powder
⅔ cup milk

Beat egg whites with sugar until stiff peaks form then set aside. Cream shortening, add salt and vanilla, and then gradually add sugar. Add egg yolks one at a time and beat until light and creamy. Take a small amount of flour and gently toss with the huckleberries to coat them and set them aside. The flour will keep them from settling down to the bottom.

Sift remaining flour with baking powder and add to batter. Alternate with milk. Fold in beaten egg whites and the huckleberries. Pour batter in a greased 8x11" pan. Lightly sprinkle top with sugar and bake at 350 degrees for 50-60 minutes.

Aunt VJ's Banana Cake

1 box white cake mix
1 cup bananas
2 eggs
¼ cup oil
¾ tsp. baking soda
1 tsp. baking powder
1 cup water

Mix together dry ingredients in a large mixing bowl. In a separate bowl, mix ½ cup of bananas with 1 cup water. Slowly add the mixed water and bananas to the dry ingredients along with the oil and eggs. Mix well then slowly add the remaining ½ cup of bananas. Pour mixture in a cake pan and bake at 350 degrees for 30-35 minutes.

Icing for the Banana Cake

2 Tbs. flour
½ cup milk
½ cup sugar
¾ cup powdered sugar
½ cup butter
1 tsp. vanilla

Mix flour and milk to make a paste and set aside. Add ½ cup sugar and butter. Mix for 5-10 minutes until sugar is dissolved then add the mixture of flour and paste along with the vanilla. Mix well and slowly add the powdered sugar until the mixture is easily spreadable. Cut cake in half and spread in between cake layers. Frost the cake with remaining icing.

Joe's Rum cake

1½ cups sugar
2 eggs
2 Tbs. heavy cream
⅛ level teaspoon salt
1 cup sifted flour + 2 heaping Tbs. of flour
1½ teaspoon baking powder
1 tsp. vanilla
½ cup hot (not boiled) milk
Butter (to grease cake pan)

Mix sugar, eggs, heavy cream, and salt until smooth. Slowly add flour, baking powder, and vanilla—mix well. Slowly add hot milk. Mix well and immediately pour mixture into a buttered cake pan. Do not allow the milk to cool. Immediately place into a preheated 360 degree oven and bake for 30 minutes or until a toothpick inserted comes out clear. While the cake is baking, prepare the rum sauce (noted below). When the cake is finished cooking, remove from the oven and remove the cake from the pan by transferring it to a slightly larger cake pan. Let the cake cool down until it is just warm. Pour the rum sauce over the cake, loosely cover with wax paper, and let sit overnight.

The rum sauce

1½ cups white sugar
1 cup cold water
⅓ cup dark rum

Boil water and sugar for about three minutes. Remove from heat and allow to cool. Once cool, add the rum and let stand.

Almond icing for rum cake

½ pint whipping cream
⅓ cup sugar
1 ⅓ teaspoons almond flavoring

Whip ingredients together until stiff. Cut the rum cake into squares and top with the icing.

Carolee's Rum cake

1 cup chopped nuts
1 yellow cake mix
13.4 ounce package instant vanilla pudding
4 eggs
½ cup cold milk
½ cup vegetable oil
½ cup Meyers Rum

Pre heat oven to 325 degrees, in a mixing bowl mix cake mix, vanilla pudding, eggs, milk, oil and rum, beat for 2 minutes. Grease a Bundt pan and sprinkle the chopped nuts into it. Pour the batter into the Bundt pan and bake for about 1 hour. Cool in pan and invert onto serving platter.

Glaze

½ cup butter
¼ cup water
1 cup sugar
½ cup Meyers Dark Rum

In pan mix water, butter and sugar and boil for 5 minutes remove from stove and slowly pour in the dark rum stir well. Poke holes into the top of the cake and spoon glaze over the top and sprinkle with powder sugar.

Carolee's Monkey Bread

16-18 frozen yeast rolls (Not thawed)
1 small package regular butterscotch pudding
1 cup chopped pecans
½ cup brown sugar
1 stick butter

Grease a Bundt pan and place frozen rolls into pan. Open pudding and sprinkle over the rolls, then sprinkle the brown sugar. Melt the butter and then pour over the rolls, sprinkle with the chopped pecans. Set on the counter and cover with a damp towel. Allow to rise for 8-10 hours, Place in preheated 350 degree oven and bake for 30 minutes. When done remove and allow to slightly cool and then invert onto serving plate. Drizzle with Carmel sauce.

Campfire Peaches

1 1-quart can of peaches, halved or quarter cut
3-4 shots of whiskey

Open the can and drink just enough of the peach juice to pour in the whiskey. Stir then eat the peaches and slurp the juice. Some might say the campfire is optional.

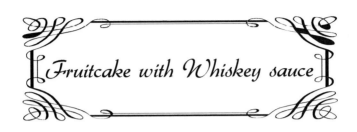

Fruitcake with Whiskey Sauce

½ lb. dried cranberries
½ lb. dried blueberries
1 lb. unsalted butter at room temperature
2¼ cups sugar
4 oz. almond paste
8 eggs
1 cup Grand Marnier liqueur
4 cups all-purpose flour
2 tsp. baking powder
¼ tsp. salt
¼ tsp. ground cinnamon
⅛ tsp. freshly grated nutmeg
1 cup pecan pieces
1 cup walnut pieces
1 cup chopped macadamia nuts
½ cup bourbon

Simple Syrup

2 cups sugar
2 cups water
Zest and juice from 2 lemons

Make the simple syrup by combining sugar and water in a medium-size heavy-bottomed saucepan over medium-high heat. Add the lemon zest and juice and bring to a boil, stirring to dissolve the sugar. Boil for 2 minutes and remove from the heat. Combine the dried fruits together and add to the simple syrup. Let steep for 5 minutes. Strain and reserve the syrup.

Using an electric mixer fitted with a paddle, cream the butter, sugar, and almond paste at low speed, occasionally scraping down the sides of the bowl. Beat until the mixture is fluffy and smooth. Add eggs one at a time, mixing in between each addition on low speed, and scraping down the sides of the bowl as necessary. Mix in ½ cup of Grand Marnier. Combine the flour, baking powder, salt, cinnamon, and nutmeg in a medium-sized bowl and blend well. Add this mixture to the butter mixture a little at a time with the mixer on low speed-making sure each time the mixing becomes smooth. Continue to scrape down the sides of the bowl as necessary. The batter should be thick at this point. Add the soaked fruit and all the nuts a little at a time, mixing well. Scrape down the sides of the bowl and the paddle.

Pre-heat the oven to 350 degrees. Lightly grease 1 large Bunt cake pan and spoon the batter into the pan. Bake until golden and a toothpick inserted comes out clean. Cool for 10 minutes in the pan then remove the cake completely onto a wire rack. Allow cake to become stale for 3-4 days, and then gently put the cake back into the cake pan.

Combine the simple syrup with the remaining ½ cup Grand Marnier and bourbon. Using a tablespoon, pour about 4 tablespoons over the cake once every 2-3 days until all of the syrup is used. Let the cake age for up to 3 weeks before eating.

Whiskey Sauce

3 cups heavy cream
½ cup bourbon
½ cup sugar
2¼ tablespoons cornstarch

Combine 2¾ cups of the cream with the bourbon and sugar in a medium-size nonstick saucepan over medium heat. Stir to dissolve the sugar. In a small bowl, dissolve the cornstarch in the remaining ¼ cup cream. Add this to the cream and bourbon mixture and simmer, stirring often until the mixture thickens. Remove from the heat and serve warm with the fruitcake.

Nut Brittle

2 cups water
4 cups sugar
2 cups corn syrup
2 Tbs. pure cane syrup
2 tsp. salt
4 cups mixed nuts (pecans, cashews and macadamia nuts)
¼ cup unsalted butter
½ teaspoon baking soda

Line two baking sheets with parchment paper. Combine water and sugar in a large nonstick heavy-bottomed saucepan over medium-high heat. Stir to dissolve the sugar. Add the corn syrup, cane syrup, and salt and stir constantly and slowly with a wooden spoon until the mixture comes to a gentle boil (about 12 minutes). Continue stirring until the mixture reaches between 225-230 degrees on a candy thermometer. Add the nuts and continue stirring until the mixture reaches 290 degrees. Remove the pan from the heat. Add butter and baking soda and stir until the butter is completely melted. Pour the mixture onto the baking sheets and spread evenly with a rubber spatula. Let cool completely. Break into pieces and store in an airtight container.

Pocket Cakes

2 cups flour
2 cups oatmeal
1 cup brown sugar
½ tsp. salt
½ tsp. baking soda
½ lb. butter, softened

Filling

1 lb. dried blueberries or chopped dates.
1 cup brown sugar
1 cup hot water

Mix together all of the cake ingredients except butter. Cut pieces of butter into the dry mixture, working and mixing with fingers until a uniform dough has been created.

Cook the filling ingredients in a saucepan or small skillet just until you have a uniform mixture. Let cool.

Spread half of the dough on the bottom of a pie pan. Cover with the cooled filling then spread the remainder of the crumb dough on top. Bake in a moderate oven for 25-30 minutes. Cool then cut into squares (similar to fudge or wedges). Put a couple in your shirt pocket and head outdoors.

Huckleberry Cobbler

4 cups fresh or frozen huckleberries
1 cup water
¾ cup sugar
2 Tbs. butter
3 Tbs. cornstarch

Cake Batter

4 oz. butter
2 cups flour
1½ cup sugar
¼ tsp. salt
2½ Tbs. baking powder
1 ⅓ cup milk

Preheat oven to 350 degrees. Boil water then add berries and butter and bring to a boil again. Mix cornstarch and sugar together and stir into berries. Cook until sugar is dissolved and starts to thicken. Remove from heat.

Cream butter and sugar then add milk. Sift together flour, baking powder, and salt. Stir dry ingredients into creamed mixture. Pour cake batter into the bottom of a pan, and then spoon berries on top. Bake for approximately 50 minutes or until the cake rises above the berries and becomes golden brown.

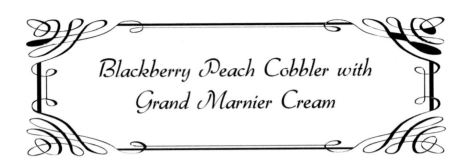

Blackberry Peach Cobbler with Grand Marnier Cream

¼ cup sugar
¼ cup brown sugar
1 Tbs. cornstarch
½ cup water
1 Tbs. lemon juice
2 Tbs. Grand Marnier
2 cups peaches peeled and sliced
1 cup blackberries fresh or frozen
1 cup flour sifted
½ cup sugar
1½ tsp. baking powder
½ tsp. salt
½ cup milk
¼ cup butter softened
2 Tbs. sugar
¼ tsp. nutmeg

Grand Marnier Cream

1 cup whipping cream
1 tablespoon powdered sugar
1 tablespoon Grand Marnier

Preheat oven to 375 degrees. In a saucepan, combine ¼ cup sugar, brown sugar, and cornstarch. Add water and blend well. Cook over medium heat, stirring constantly until thick. Add lemon juice, Grand Marnier, peaches, and blackberries. Turn into a 2-quart baking dish.

In a mixing bowl, sift together flour, ½ cup sugar, baking powder, and salt. Add milk and softened butter and beat until smooth. Spoon over cobbler and bake for 40-45 minutes or until lightly browned. Let cool and serve with Grand Marnier cream.

To make the cream, whip cream until foamy. Add sugar and Grand Marnier and whip until thick but not stiff.

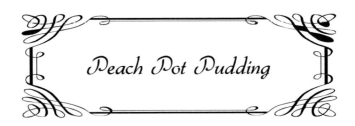

Peach Pot Pudding

Apricots, apples, pears, berries, or cherries (heck, any fresh fruit will
    work, but peaches are my favorite)
2 cups fresh peaches diced ½"
1 cup sugar
1 cup flour
2 tsp. baking powder
½ tsp. salt
½ cup milk
½ cup brown sugar
1 tsp. nutmeg
½ tsp. cinnamon
1 Tbs. butter
1 cup hot water

Sift together ½ cup of sugar and flour, baking powder, and salt. Stir
in milk to form a smooth batter then add diced peaches and mix well.
Grease the bottom and sides of a Dutch oven heavily and pour the batter
into it. Combine the remaining ½ cup sugar with brown sugar, nutmeg,
and cinnamon. Rub it into the butter and pour hot water over it. Stir
until the butter and sugar are dissolved then pour into the Dutch oven
over the batter. Close the oven and bury it in coals for 45 minutes. If
using a kitchen oven, use a deep-dish open pan and cook at 325 degrees
for 30 minutes.

Dutch Oven Apple Cobbler

3 cups apples peeled and sliced
1½ cups fine dry breadcrumbs or graham cracker crumbs
½ cup melted butter
1½ cups brown sugar
1½ Tbs. cinnamon
1 tsp. nutmeg
½ tsp. powdered cloves
½ cup lemon juice

Mix crumbs and butter. Grease the sides and bottom of the Dutch oven then press the crumbs thickly on the bottom and sides to form a crust, Mix sugar and spices together. Peel and core the apples and slice about ¼-½" thick. Put a layer of apples on the bottom of the pan, sprinkle with brown sugar, sugar and spice mixture, and a few drops of lemon juice. Add layers of apple slices until all apples are used, sprinkling between each layer with the spiced sugar and lemon juice. Spread a thick layer of the buttered crumbs on top of the last layer of apples and dot with butter. Close the Dutch oven, bury in coals, and cook for 30-40 minutes. Serve in bowls with cold cream poured over the top. This can be cooked in the kitchen using an uncovered pan. Heat oven to 300 degrees and cook for 30 minutes.

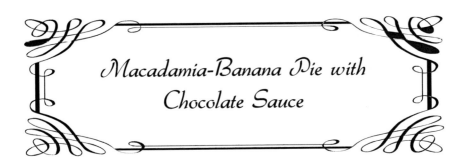

Macadamia-Banana Pie with Chocolate Sauce

9" pie shell baked and cooled
⅔ cup sugar
¼ cup cornstarch
½ tsp. salt
3 cups milk
4 egg yolks
2 Tbs. butter
1 Tbs. vanilla
½ cup macadamia nuts roasted and chopped

Garnish

1 large banana
Sliced macadamia nuts
Chocolate curls

In a 3-quart saucepan, mix sugar, cornstarch, and salt. Using a wire whip, blend milk and egg yolks in a medium bowl. Gradually stir the egg mixture into the cornstarch mixture. Stirring constantly, cook over medium heat until the mixture thickens and boils. Boil and stir vigorously for 1 minute. Remove from heat and slowly add butter and vanilla while stirring.

Press plastic wrap onto the surface of the filling in the saucepan or transfer filling to a cool mixing bowl and press with plastic wrap. Cool to room temperature.

Sprinkle Macadamia nuts in the bottom of the pie shell and top with banana. Pour cooled filling carefully over layers. Chill for at least 2 hours.

Chocolate Sauce

⅔ cups sugar divided in thirds
½ cup cold water
4 oz. unsweetened chocolate chopped into large pieces
½ cup heavy cream
1 tsp. vanilla

In a small, heavy saucepan stir together ⅓ cup sugar and water. Bring to boil over high heat. Reduce heat to low and simmer 1 minute. Remove from heat.

In a food processor or heavy-duty blender, process ⅓ cup sugar and chocolate in bursts until the mixture is ground finely. While processor or blender is running, pour hot syrup through feed opening in a slow stream. Without stopping the machine, add cream and vanilla. Process for about 30 seconds.

To serve, pour some chocolate sauce on the bottom of a serving plate, add a slice of pie, then drizzle more chocolate sauce on top. Garnish with macadamia nut and chocolate curl

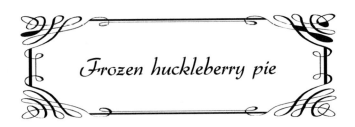

Frozen huckleberry pie

1 lb. frozen huckleberries
2 egg whites
1 cup sugar
1 Tbs. lemon juice
½ pint heavy cream
1 9" pie shell cooked and cooled
Fresh huckleberries (for garnish)

In a large chilled bowl, combine berries, egg whites, sugar, and lemon juice. Beat on high speed for 10 minutes until firm and frothy. Whip cream until stiff peaks form and fold into the berry mixture. Spoon into the pie shell and freeze for at least 8 hours. Garnish with fresh huckleberries when serving.

Chocolate Bourbon Pecan Pie Bars

3 cups flour
2 cups sugar divided
1 cup butter softened
½ teaspoon salt
1¼ cup pure cane syrup
¼ cup bourbon
4 eggs beaten
1½ teaspoons vanilla
3 cups pecans chopped

Preheat oven to 350 degrees. Grease the bottom and sides of a 9x13" baking pan. In a large mixing bowl, beat flour, ½ cup sugar, butter, and salt at medium speed until mixture resembles coarse crumbs. Press firmly and evenly into the pan. Bake for 20 minutes.

Meanwhile, stir cane syrup and chocolate over low heat in a 3-quart saucepan until chocolate melts. Remove from heat. Stir in bourbon, remaining sugar, eggs, and vanilla until blended. Stir in pecans. Pour over crust and spread evenly. Bake for 30 minutes or until the filling is firm around the edges. Let cool before cutting.

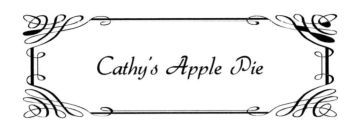

Cathy's Apple Pie

Growing up, my younger sister was well known for her cooking skills—not because the food was good, but because she somehow managed to burn everything, including water. I'm not kidding—she burned a pot of water! Later in life, though, she figured out how to make apple pie and I have to say she learned it well.

1 double piecrust
6 medium apples, peeled, cored, and thinly sliced
1½ tablespoons lemon juice
⅓ cup packed brown sugar
⅓ cup sugar
½ Tbs. cornstarch
⅛ tsp. salt
¾ tsp. ground cinnamon
¼ tsp. nutmeg
1½ Tbs. butter

Preheat oven to 450 degrees. Line a 9" pie plate with one piecrust. Place sliced apples in a bowl and sprinkle lemon juice over apples. In a small mixing bowl, combine sugars, cornstarch, salt, cinnamon, and nutmeg. Mix then add to apples. Mix well and pour into the piecrust. Level it out and place other piecrust on top and seal edges. Prick the crust, or cut slits or designs to allow steam to escape during cooking. Bake for 10 minutes. Reduce temperature to 350 degrees and bake for 35-40 more minutes or until apples are tender.

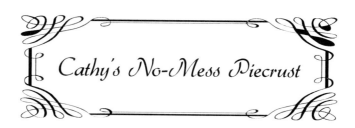

Cathy's No-Mess Piecrust

½ cup plus 2 Tbs. vegetable oil
½ cup milk
1 tsp. vinegar
2 cups all-purpose flour

Combine all ingredients at once and stir with a fork. Roll out between sheets of wax paper. Makes two 9" crusts.

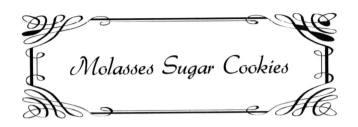

Molasses Sugar Cookies

¾ cup shortening
1 cup sugar
¼ cup molasses
1 egg
2 tsp. baking soda
2 cups flour
½ tsp. crushed cloves
1 tsp. cinnamon
½ tsp. salt
½ tsp. fresh grated ginger

Mix all ingredients together. Scoop out the dough to desired size of cookies and place on cookie sheet. Bake at 350 degrees for 10 minutes.

Sesame Cookies

4 sticks butter softened
1½ cups sugar
3 cups flour
1 cup sesame seeds
2 cups coconut
½ cup chopped pecans

Cream butter and gradually add sugar. Beat until light and fluffy. Add flour until combined. Stir in sesame seeds, coconut, and pecans until well mixed. Divide dough into thirds. Place one third on a long sheet of waxed paper and shape into a long roll (about 2"). Wrap all three rolls the same way and refrigerate until firm. Cut firmed rolls into ¼" slices and bake on ungreased cookie sheets for 15-20 minutes at 300 degrees.

Pumpkin Cookies

1 cup pumpkin
1 cup brown sugar
½ cup oil
1 tsp. vanilla
2 cups sifted flour
1 tsp. baking soda
1 tsp. baking powder
½ tsp. salt
½ tsp. cinnamon
½ tsp. nutmeg
¼ tsp. ginger
1 cup raisins
½ cup chopped nuts

Mix all ingredients together and scoop onto a greased cookie sheet. Bake at 350 for 12-15 minutes. Depending on cookie size, this recipe will make about 3-4 dozen cookies.

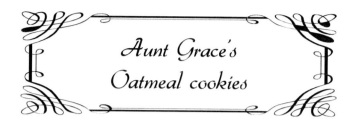

Aunt Grace's
Oatmeal cookies

2 cups shortening
2 cups brown sugar
2 cups white sugar
4 eggs
4 cups oatmeal
4 cups flour
2 tsp. baking soda
1 tsp. salt

Mix all ingredients together and let stand at least 15-20 minutes. Scoop onto greased cookie sheet and bake at 350 degrees for 10-12 minutes.

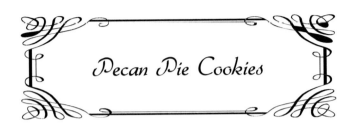

Pecan Pie Cookies

1 cup butter
½ cup sugar
½ cup pure cane syrup
2 eggs separated
2½ cups flour unsifted

Pecan Filling

½ cup powdered sugar
¼ cup butter
3 Tbs. pure cane syrup
½ cup pecans chopped

In a large bowl blend butter and sugar together using an electric mixer on low speed. Add cane syrup and egg yolks and beat until thoroughly blended. Stir in flour. Chill several hours.

To prepare pecan filling, combine powdered sugar, butter, and cane syrup in a saucepan; stir to blend. Cook over medium heat, stirring occasionally, until mixture reaches a full boil. Remove from heat and stir in pecans. Chill.

Preheat oven to 375 degrees. Beat egg whites slightly then set aside. Using 1 tablespoon of dough for each cookie, roll into balls, brushing each very lightly with egg white. Place on a greased cookie sheet, leaving a 2-inch space between cookies. Bake at 375 degrees for 5 minutes. Remove from oven then roll ½ teaspoon of the chilled pecan filling into a ball and firmly press into the center of each cookie. Bake 5 minutes longer or until lightly browned. Let cool for 5 minutes on the cookie sheet. Remove and cool completely on a rack.

Chocolate Cookies

1 cup Eagle brand sweet milk
1 stick butter
12 oz. chocolate chips
1 cup sifted flour
1 cup chopped nuts
1 tsp. vanilla

Mix milk, butter, and chocolate and put in the microwave until melted. Add flour, nuts, and vanilla. Allow to cool 10-15 minutes then drop by tablespoon on a greased cookie sheet. Bake at 350 degrees for 7-10 minutes.

Shortbread

1 cup butter
⅔ cups brown sugar
2 ⅔ cups cake flour (remove 2 Tbs. and sift the rest)

Beat the butter and brown sugar for 20 minutes then add the 2 tablespoons of unsifted flour. Slowly add the remaining sifted flour. Cut dough into thirds, roll in wax paper to about 2" in size, and place in refrigerator for about 2 hours. Cut into ¼" slices and place on a greased cookie sheet. Bake at 325 degrees for 25-30 minutes.

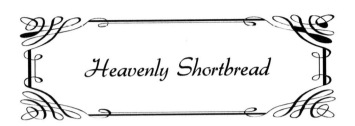

Heavenly Shortbread

2 cups butter soft
1 cup white sugar
4 cups flour
2 tsp. cornstarch

Cream butter thoroughly then slowly add sugar, flour, and cornstarch. Mix well. Press into an ungreased jelly roll pan (11 x 15 x ½"). Bake at 325 degrees for about 30 minutes or until light brown. Cut into squares while still warm.

Cornflake Cookies

1 cup butter
1 cup sugar
1 tsp. soda
1 tsp. cream of tarter
1½ cups flour
⅛ tsp. salt
1 tsp. vanilla
2 cups cornflakes (do not crush)

Mix together and let sit overnight in the refrigerator. Bake at 350 degrees for 10-12 minutes.

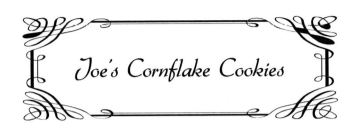

Joe's Cornflake Cookies

1 cup butter
1 cup vegetable oil
1 cup white sugar
1 cup brown sugar
1 egg
2 tsp. vanilla extract
1 cup crushed corn flakes
1 cup chopped pecans
1 cup Heath English toffee bits
1 cup quick-cooking oatmeal
4 cups flour
1 Tbs. baking soda
½ tsp. salt

Preheat oven to 325 degrees. Cream butter, sugars, vanilla, and egg. Slowly add oil; mix well. In a separate bowl, add all dry ingredients and mix well. Slowly add dry ingredients to wet until everything is combined. Form dough into walnut sized balls and place onto ungreased cookie sheets. Flatten with a fork and bake for 10-12 minutes. Remove pan and allow to cool for about 1-2 minutes. Remove to a rack to continue cooling.

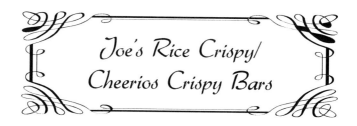

Joe's Rice Crispy/ Cheerios Crispy Bars

2 cups regular rice crispies
2 cups chocolate rice crispies
2 cups chocolate cheerios
5 Tbs. butter
1 package marshmallows

Heat butter in large pan until melted. Add marshmallows a little at a time until all are melted, making sure not to burn them. Once melted, add all the cereal a little at a time until everything is mixed. Place into a pre-buttered 9x13" dish, press flat, and allow to cool. Cut into desired serving pieces and enjoy. The cheerios makes it a heart healthy treat!

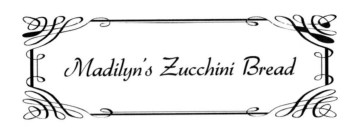

Madilyn's Zucchini Bread

3 eggs
2¼ cup sugar
2 cups shredded zucchini
1½ tsp. vanilla extract
1 cup oil
3 cups flour
½ tsp. baking powder
4 tsp. cinnamon
1 tsp. baking soda
1 tsp. salt
1 cup chopped nuts
½ cup honey

Mix the first five ingredients in a large bowl. Mix the next five ingredients in a second bowl. Mix the dry ingredients into the zucchini mixture and add the chopped nuts and honey. Grease and flour two 9x5" loaf pans then pour in the batter. Bake at 350 degrees for 1 hour. Check with a toothpick and cook longer if needed.

Smoked Meats and fish

When it comes to smoking meats, I find that the simpler the brine is, the better the product will be. Therefore, I only use two brines: a wet brine and a dry brine. I use the wet brine for birds and the dry brine for everything else. The secret to a good brine is to taste it before you put the meat into it. The brine should be salty but not to the point of making your mouth pucker up. Adjust the brine by adding equal amounts of sugar or salt depending on the initial taste test. A non-metallic container big enough to hold the meat to be smoked will also be needed. Old crocks work well, as do mid-sized coolers. The following brine recipes are enough to brine up to 20 pounds of meat.

Wet brine

1 cup Morton's tender quick salt
1 cup brown sugar
1 cup sugar
1 gallon apple cider

Dry Brine

1 cup Morton's tender quick salt
1 cup brown sugar
1 cup sugar
Coarse ground black pepper.

Smoked Turkey

1 turkey
Wet brine
1 cup brown sugar
½ lb. butter

Wash and pat dry the turkey. Prepare wet brine and submerge the turkey into the brine, making sure the turkey is completely submerged. Allow to sit for 24 hours in a cool place. When ready, remove turkey from brine and rinse and pat dry. Melt butter and brown sugar in a saucepan just until sugar is melted. Hang turkey in your smoker and rub the melted brown sugar and butter on the turkey. Smoke for 2-3 hours. Remove turkey from smoker and finish in the oven.

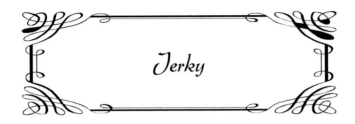

Jerky

10 pounds of meat sliced to desired size (all fat removed)
Dry brine

Place meat into the dry brine and allow to soak for 24 hours in a cool place. Remove meat from brine and rinse. Place onto rack and let drip-dry. Add cracked pepper and place into smoker. Depending on the smoker, smoke for 14-24 hours. I smoke jerky at 200 degrees for 14 hours in my smoker. When jerky is smoked remove from the smoker, place smoked jerky onto a plate in small batches, microwave for 30 seconds, then place into a container. Repeat until all of the jerky has been microwaved and is in the refrigerator. Allow to cool overnight. Note: the microwave process is optional, but I find that it seals the jerky and allows it to retain a little moisture.

Liverwurst

2 lbs. Deer or elk liver

2 lbs. pork butt (if deer or elk liver weighs more than 2 lbs. add an equal amount of pork)

1 sweet yellow onion

2 Tbs. of Tender Quick curing salt (kosher or canning salt can also be used)

1 Tbs. white fine ground pepper

½ cup powdered milk

1 tsp. allspice

1 tsp. marjoram

½ tsp. sage

4 cloves garlic

1 cup ice water

In a medium sized bowl mix the salt, pepper, allspice, marjoram, sage, and powdered milk together and set it aside. Cut liver into chunks small enough to fit into your grinder and boil it for about 20 minutes. It should still be pink—remove and allow to cool. (This can be done the night before.) Cut pork into 1" cubes, run pork and liver through grinder, then cut onion and run onion and garlic through grinder. Add ice water to the seasoning mix then add to the meat, mix all together and let sit for about 5-10 minutes. Run all ingredients back through the grinder again then stuff into 2" stuffing. Bring a large pot of water to just a boil and place stuffed sausage into water until the sausage reaches an internal temp of 152 degrees. *Apply a light smoke if desired.

Smoked Fish

When I lived in Astoria I would smoke on average 100 pounds of salmon and 100 pounds of sturgeon a year—and that was just for me. For the holidays, I would smoke the salmon fillets whole.

10 pounds of fish
Dry brine

Cut fish to the desired size of serving pieces (with the exception of smelt—I always recommend at least filleting the fish in half). Place fish into dry brine and allow to soak for 24 hours. Remove from brine and rinse. Place on racks and allow to drip-dry. Add cracked pepper to fish, place in the smoker, and smoke for 14-24 hours depending on the smoker. Remove from the smoker in small batches, place the smoked fish onto a plate, and microwave for 20-30 seconds. Repeat in small batches until all pieces are microwaved. Place in the refrigerator and allow to cool.

Canadian Bacon

10-20 lbs. whole pork loin or bear loin
Dry brine
Cracked pepper
Container large enough to hold the pork loin (I use a large Tupperware container with a lid and cut the loin in half to fit)

Add the pork loins to the dry brine, making sure all sides are covered. Place into container and place in a cool place. Allow to brine for 7 days, rolling the loins over once a day. After brining, remove and place onto racks and allow to dry. For peppered bacon add cracked pepper. Smoke for 3-6 hours and remove. Allow to cool then cut into 1-pound sections and freeze.

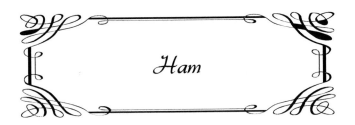

Ham

Shoulder from bear or pork
Dry brine to cover

Large Tupperware container or a salt box (optional: make a wooden box from cedar or fir—it should be big enough to hold a 20-pound ham or at least 2 full slabs of bacon with salt)

Trim the shoulder, leaving a small amount of fat, and add a layer of prepared dry brine in the bottom of the salt box. Place the ham into the box, cover with remaining brine, and allow to cure for 7-14 days (I have let them cure for up to a year) in a cool place—the temperature should not go above 50 degrees. After curing, remove from cure and rinse and hang in the smoker. Smoke at 150 degrees for 10-12 hours. The ham can now be cooked or frozen until ready to cook.

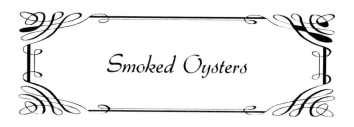

Smoked Oysters

1 gallon of shucked oysters
Salted water

Place water in large pot and bring to a gentle boil. Add Oysters long enough for them to firm up and then remove and place on racks, allow the oysters to dry and then place into smoker and smoke for about 1-2 hours.

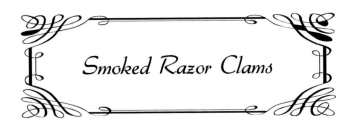

Smoked Razor Clams

1 lb. cleaned razor clams (frozen clams also work well)
Salted water

Heat 4 quarts of water to a boil in a large stockpot. Add clams and cook for no more than 2 minutes. Remove clams and place on smoking racks. Allow them to dry, and then place in the smoker for 1-2 hours.

CPSIA information can be obtained at www.ICGtesting.com
Printed in the USA
BVOW07s0134260713

326855BV00002B/173/P